For James Universal McCorquodale
whose coming into this world
gave me the idea for this book.
DM

Illustrated Children's Books

black dog
publishing

london uk

Contents

Contemporary Children's Books

Authors and Illustrators 1945–Now

Afterwords

A Big Thank You

Foreword

Anthony Browne

Anthony Browne is an award-winning and highly respected author/illustrator. In 2009, he was made sixth Children's Laureate, replacing Michael Rosen, and becoming only the second illustrator to hold the post since Quentin Blake. The Children's Laureate is an ambassadorial role for children's literature, and Browne pledged to use the opportunity to reinvest the picture-book with greater importance—not just as a genre exclusively for small children.

It was Alice in Wonderland who asked, "What is the use of a book without pictures or conversation?" and as an author and illustrator of children's books, I'm inclined to agree with her. There is a terrible pressure on children to leave pictures behind and grow into words, as though this is an essential part of education and maturity. But I strongly believe that the ability to read images is as equally important as the ability to read words.

The illustrations in children's books are the first paintings most children see and because of that they are incredibly important. What we see and share at that age stays with us for life. In the best picture-books the illustrations tell as much of the story as the words. These illustrations don't just happen by chance—the placing of figures in space and in relation to others, the use of colour and light all help to express emotion and tell the story. It is this aspect of picture-books that fascinates me; the gap between the image and the words, the gap which has to be filled by the reader's imagination.

Learning how to look is a skill we don't value highly enough. Watch people in an art museum and see how quickly they walk past each painting on their way to buy reproductions in the gift shop. To see and understand a work of art takes time and patience. It is often said that we live in a visual age, and indeed children are bombarded with visual imagery through television, video, cinema and computers, but these are all fast moving images allowing no time for reflection. Looking takes time.

Children generally have a much higher developed visual awareness than adults. Many of my illustrations have hidden details, images which tell parts of the story that the words don't tell us, and kids are far quicker to spot these details than adults who often take pictures for granted. What happens to this visual awareness? Where do we lose it between childhood and adulthood? All children can draw, but how many adults can? I believe that much is lost when we encourage children to leave pictures and illustrated books behind. I feel it is no coincidence that this happens at about the same time that children stop drawing with the natural creativity that all of them possess.

It is perhaps a fairly obvious thing to repeat but a picture can paint a thousand words, and the neglect of them will lead us to become even more visually illiterate than we already are. We hear much concern about the problems of verbal illiteracy amongst our children but when did you last hear anyone worrying about visual illiteracy?

Illustrations in books enhance the enjoyment of reading, and it's only through the enjoyment of reading that we will create true readers—readers who will love books.

Illustration © 1988 Anthony Browne. From *Alice's Adventures in Wonderland* by Lewis Carroll and illustrated by Anthony Browne. Reproduced by permission of Walker Books Ltd, London SE11 5HJ.

The World in Pictures

Peter Hunt

Children's books are probably the most diverse, inventive, and fascinating of literary forms not only for children but for adults—not least because childhood changes, and adults, looking back on the kaleidoscope of time, or down on the childhoods around them, see the books through refracting prisms.

Like children, 'children's books' are not some amorphous mass. There are classics—as Alan Bennett called them, books that "everyone is assumed to have read and often thinks they have", like *The Wind in the Willows*; there are 'household' books that everyone has read, such as *Winnie the Pooh*; there are serious novels, such as Philip Pullman's *His Dark Materials* trilogy; best-selling middle-of-the-road books and the endless series of popular mass-produced fodder. Virtually every adult genre is represented and, if children's lists are rather light on crime and punishment, there are books with challenging, apparently adult, themes that are nonetheless adopted by children, such as Anna Sewell's *Black Beauty*, 1877, and numerous folk and fairy tales. As Tolkien said: "Children as a class—and except in a common lack of experience they are not one—neither like fairy-stories more, nor understand them better than adults do...."

And there is the phenomenal library of illustrated books (where pictures complement the text) and picture-books (where the pictures come first, or are more-than-equal partners). Children's books have always led the way in blending words and pictures, and recently the polymorphic power of this blend has been recognised by—and appropriated by—adults, in the

Opposite *Old King Cole's Book of Nursery Rhymes*, 1901, engraved and printed in colour by Edmund Evans after J Byam Shaw, courtesy The Wandsworth Collection.
Above Illustration from *Chatterbox*, November 18, 1875, courtesy Moira Allen.

form of graphic novels and multi-media texts. Even the lowly comic is being recognised as a 'legitimate' art form.

Add to that a 250 year old backlist in Britain alone, an uncountable output from countries all over the world, 'crossover' books and computer 'games'—and we have an astonishing array of material to enjoy.

Not surprisingly, then, children's books are not simple —as Ursula K Le Guin said: "Sure it's simple, writing for kids. Just as simple as bringing them up"—and, whatever some adults might like to think, they cannot possibly be innocent. The history of children's books is inevitably bound up with the history of culture, society, and ideology: children's books might portray society as it wishes itself to be or as it wishes to be seen, but they cannot stand outside it.

They are written by adults who are trying to negotiate meaning with a less-experienced or differently experienced group of readers, whose likes and responses are difficult to fathom. To say that we know what children like is a rash generalisation—and, after all, they can only like or dislike what they are given: manipulation, benign or otherwise is inevitable. And can children resist this manipulation, or are they helpless victims of adults' intentions?

For adults, children's books are more difficult to read than are adults' books: do we read them for our adult-selves, or our child-selves: or do we read them on behalf of children, so that we can influence what they do, or protect them from what we think they should not see? And if we censor children's books (Beatrix Potter's publisher was not at all happy about all Tom Kitten's clothes falling off; evangelical critics in around the world today want to ban any reference to sexuality), who are we protecting: the children, or ourselves and our ideal of childhood?

Nor should we underestimate how difficult even the 'simplest' children's book is to read. We assume, for example, that picture-books are easy to read. Johann Amos Comenius, who produced what is arguably the first picture-book in the Western tradition, the *Orbis Sensualium Pictus* published in England in 1659 as *Visible World; or, A Nomenclature, and Pictures of all the Chief Things that are in the World, and of Man's Enjoyment Therein*, with its 150 woodcuts, wrote that "pictures are the most intelligible books that children can look upon". That might seem obvious, but if we look carefully at what seem to be the simplest of books—such as Roger Hargreaves' mega-selling *Mister Men* books—we should see that they depend on a highly abstract and symbolic form of art, which requires remarkably sophisticated interpretation. Put pictures next to words and you have a cornucopia of interpretative possibilities. Pictures, unlike words, are not read linearly: they communicate by codes of shape, colour, texture, symbolism, and juxtaposition; they depend upon complex assumptions about visual conventions. Equally, just as all children's books are inevitably influenced by their cultural context, so illustrated books and picture-books absorb and reflect the world of art that surrounds them. A comparison of the realism of black and white illustrators like HR Millar in the 1890s, the Art Deco of the European-influenced books of the 1930s and today's postmodernist work by Lauren Child or Lane Smith makes the point. Picture-books are sophisticated members of the literary-artistic culture.

The history of illustrated books and picture-books parallels the history of children's books, but it is also closely linked to the history of printing. The use of woodcuts in the earliest books developed through the nineteenth century into sophisticated wood and metal engraving, allowing the vast majority of children's books and magazines to have monochrome pictures. It was not until the end of the century that high-quality colour printing became available, and with it the first picture-books as we now know them. In the 1920s and 1930s, the increased sophistication of offset lithography was seized upon by a group of experimental artists, while after the Second World War, photolithography and, later, digital imaging meant that any pictures could be reproduced to the highest standard and in large numbers. It was then that the picture-book really came into its own.

Astrid Lindgren

Pippi

Longstocking

Illustrated by Lauren Child

Fabulous Histories, or The History of the Robins, for the Instruction of Children, on their Treatment of Animals, by Mrs Trimmer, illustrated by Harrison Weir, courtesy of The Wandsworth Collection.

The Earliest Illustrated Books

Adults and children shared the earliest printed texts, which included William Caxton's version of *Aesop's Fables*, 1484, but there was a rapid growth of cheap educational 'chapbooks' and serious religious books such as John Bunyan's *A Book for Boys and Girls; or County Rhymes for Children*, 1686. Possibly the most famous is Isaac Watts', *Divine Songs Attempted in Easy Language for the Use of Children*, 1715; a typical verse is "Against Idleness and Mischief", which begins:

How doth the little busy bee Improve each shining hour, And gather honey all the day From every opening flower!

Divine and Moral Songs for Children, by Isaac Watts, courtesy of The Wandsworth Collection.

Books of this period were illustrated by woodcuts—very often crude, and very often used in different books with varying degrees of applicability—but we should not measure their impact from the media-saturated viewpoint of today. Simple educational pamphlets, enlivened by woodcuts, the chapbooks, were sold in their thousands by itinerant peddlers, or 'chapmen'. There was also a strong tradition of domestic book-making: the most famous survivals have been the collection of miniature books, card sets and crib-mobiles made by Jane Johnson of Witham Manor in Lincolnshire in the 1740s. The history of commercial children's books began in the mid-eighteenth century—and in this, Britain was one of the world leaders. To take a random sample, American children's books were initially imports from Britain, the first children's books in Italy date from 1768, in Slovakia and Austria from the late eighteenth century, in Spain and Brazil from the late nineteenth century, and in Iran and China from early in the twentieth century.

The most famous of these early British books is *A Little Pretty Pocket-Book*, published by the energetic John Newbery (or Jack Whirler, as Dr Johnson called him) in 1744. It demonstrates that, from the very beginning, children's books were gender-tailored commodities: the title-page reads: "Intended for the Instruction and Amusement of Little Master Tommy and pretty Miss Polly, with... a Ball and a Pincushion, the Use of which will Infallibly make Tommy a Good Boy and Polly a Good Girl."

The early commercial publishers—and many followed Newbery's lead—produced books that tried to balance commercialism and religious acceptability. They were opposed by a formidable regiment of evangelical tractarians such as Anna Laetitia Barbauld and Sarah Trimmer who flooded the market with pious reading for children. Trimmer's *The Guardian of Education*, for example (which ran from 1802 to 1806), contained "memoirs of modern philosophers both Christian and infidel... also Abstracts of Sermons on some of the most important points of Christian Doctrine". Fantasy was frowned on and, when Sarah Trimmer found herself writing *Fabulous Histories: Designed for the Instruction of Children, Respecting their Treatment of Animals*—which was a best-seller well into the nineteenth century, and which featured a family of birds that talked to each other, she could not resist a stern preface explaining that the book did not contain "the real conversation of Birds (for that it is impossible we should ever understand)".

From The Butterfly's Ball and the Grasshopper's Feast to Alice in Wonderland

The stage was set for a century-long battle between religious and educational discipline and secular liberalism and romanticism. As Charles Lamb complained to Samuel Taylor Coleridge in 1802: "Mrs Barbauld's stuff has banished all the old classics of the nursery.... Think what you would have been now, if instead of being fed with tales and old wives' fables in childhood, you had been crammed with geography and history." Gradually, children came to be seen as, if not born 'trailing clouds of glory', at least not as being sinners from the womb.

Better printing techniques allowed more lively illustrations: one of the most famous picture-books of the early nineteenth century was William Roscoe's *The Butterfly's Ball and the Grasshopper's Feast*,

1807, illustrated by William Mulready and produced using hand-coloured copper-plate engravings. The woodblocks used in the earliest children's books were improved upon towards the end of the eighteenth century by Thomas Bewick's method of hardwood engraving and George Baxter's colour printing using a metal plate for the basic image, and then over-printing colours from wood blocks. But the most significant development was Alois Senefelder's invention of

lithography, where the ink sticks to greasy areas drawn onto a 'stone' or metal plate, and is then transferred to the paper; one of the earliest examples of the use of this technique is Thomas Love Peacock's *Sir Hornbook; or, Childe Launcelot's Expedition*, 1814.

At first, nineteenth century children's books were dominated by moral tales such as Mary Martha Sherwood's *The History of the Fairchild Family, or, the Child's Manual: being a Collection of Stories Calculated to Shew the Importance and Effects of a Religious Education*, 1818, with sequels in 1842 and 1847—often illustrated with uncompromising pictures of punishments. Gradually, these were superseded by more liberal books such Catherine Sinclair's *Holiday House*, 1839, while the pious cautionary verses that dominated children's verse were challenged by Heinrich Hoffmann's satirical *Struwwelpeter [Slovenly Peter]; or, Pretty Stories and Funny Pictures for Little Children* (translated into English in 1848) which included "The Dreadful Story about Harriet and the Matches" and "The Story of Augustus Who Would Not have Any Soup" (both die, of course). This was originally printed by lithography, and hand-coloured. Another highly influential book produced by lithography (with mixed results) was Edward Lear's *A Book of Nonsense*, 1846 and 1861, which seemed, on the surface at least, to offer children nothing but fun.

Opposite top *The Butterfly's Ball and the Grasshopper's Feast,* illustrated by William Mulready.
Opposite bottom *A Book of Nonsense* by Edward Lear.
Left *The English Struwwelpeter or, Pretty Stories and Funny Pictures For Little Children*, by Heinrich Hoffmann.
All images courtesy of The Wandsworth Collection.

Illustrations © 1979, Shirley Hughes, from *Up and Up* by Shirley Hughes. Reproduced by permission of the artist.

Other stimuli for change included the appearance in 1823 and 1826 of the Grimms' *German Popular Stories*, illustrated by George Cruikshank, who is often regarded as the father of the modern picture-book. He also produced the 'Fairy Library'—four volumes, 1853–1864, which was attacked by Charles Dickens in "Frauds on the Fairies" for preaching total abstinence. From around the mid-century books for boys and for girls diverged; boys read adventures such RM Ballantyne's *The Coral Island*, 1858, and school stories such as Thomas Hughes, *Tom Brown's Schooldays*, 1857, and FW Farrar's infamously pious (and sadistic), *Eric, or Little by Little*, 1858 (notably illustrated by Gordon Browne in 1899). Illustrated magazines such as *The Boys of England* (from 1866) and imperialist writers like GA Henty—whose books are now collected for their illustrated and embossed covers—extolled the virtues of empire-building. As a Dutch commentator, R van Eeghen noted sardonically in *The Captain*, in May 1908: "After fourteen or fifteen years' perusal of [these books], the young Englishman leaves home and country with the very firm idea in his head that he, personally, is equal to two or more Frenchmen... about four Germans, an indefinite number of Russians, and any quantity you care to mention of the remaining scum of the earth."

All of this was backed up by a huge output from 'penny dreadfuls' and magazines—which inspired the Religious Tract Society to found *The Boys' Own Paper* in 1879 as an antidote. The boldly illustrated front pages of that magazine commonly featured upright British boys winning football matches or triumphing (piously) over foreign enemies.

By 1884, its companion, *The Girls' Own Paper* was reputed to have the largest circulation of any British illustrated magazine. Girls at first were given domestic stories, often with strong religious or charitable overtones, such as Hesba Stretton's *Jessica's First Prayer*, 1867, in which a beggar girl confronts the prejudices of middle class churchgoers. It is perhaps not surprising that when fantastic literature blossomed at the end of the century with writers like Mrs Molesworth and George MacDonald it centred on the girls' market, where escape from 'luxurious captivity' was itself still something of a fantasy.

Also in the mid-century two streams of illustration appeared: the 'black-and-white men', producing a very high standard of black-and-white illustrations for children's books and the popular press, and the coloured picture-book. The tradition of illustrating children's novels with line drawings survived into the 1960s, with artists such as Margery Gill, Victor Ambrus, C Walter Hodges and Shirley Hughes. Among the outstanding artists of the nineteenth century was Richard Doyle who designed the cover of *Punch*, 1843, illustrated *Fairy Tales from all Nations*, 1849, and one of the first original fairy tales, John Ruskin's *The King of the Golden River*, 1851.

These illustrators were helped by the establishment of very high-quality wood-engraving houses following the tradition of Thomas Bewick, notably the Dalziel brothers (George, Edward, Thomas, and John) who engraved *Alice's Adventures in Wonderland*, 1863—one of the first books in the first 'golden age' of children's books.

The Story of Jack and the Bean-stalk. Edited and illustrated by George Cruikshank, courtesy The Wandsworth Collection.

The Golden Age 1860–1910

A round 1860, there was a 'perfect storm' for the creation of children's books. There were radical changes in attitudes to children: medicine was improving, families were growing smaller, and individual children were more valued; there were radical changes in society, uncertainty about empire, feminism, politics, religion; and technology, from the motor car to the improvements in the printing of picture-books was changing the world.

Into these turbulent waters stepped Lewis Carroll, with one of the most famous, most quoted, most translated, and most interpreted of children's books, *Alice's Adventures in Wonderland*. Not only did this book change the tone of voice used in children's books, it integrated the illustrations into the verbal text as an equal partner—Carroll's choice of the pre-eminent

"Fury said to
a mouse, That
he met in the
house, 'Let
us both go
to law: *I*
will prose-
cute *you*.—
Come, I'll
take no de-
nial: We
must have
the trial;
For really
this morn-
ing I've
nothing
to do.'
Said the
mouse to
the cur.
'Such a
trial, dear
Sir. With
no jury
or judge,
would
be wast-
ing our
breath.'
'I'll be
judge.
I'll be
jury,'
said
cun-
ning
old
Fury:
'I'll
try
the
whole
cause,
and
con-
demn
you to
death.'"

political cartoonist of the day, John Tenniel, who worked extensively for *Punch*, was no accident. Carroll and Tenniel collaborated closely, so that the pictures added another level to the already complex texture of references, but although Tenniel, master of subtle drawings, and served well by his engravers, is perhaps the most famous of the illustrators of the period, he was not alone.

Alice's Adventures was essentially a book for girls, an inward-looking fantasy of escape, and the girls' story, which had long contained fairy-story elements, increasingly overlapped with stories which combined adult wish-fulfilment with the romantic cult of the

Opposite and above *Alice's Adventures in Wonderland*,
by Lewis Carroll, illustrations by John Tenniel, courtesy of
The Wandsworth Collection.

beautiful child. Typical of these is Frances Hodgson Burnett's *Little Lord Fauntleroy*, 1886, and it is some indication of the power of such books that Reginald Birch's illustrations of Fauntleroy's golden curls, velvet suit, and lace collar were immensely influential for boys' fashions. E Nesbit, another writer whose books are still read, married family life to fantasy, and the fantasy was made the more plausible by the realist style of her illustrators, notably HR Millar—who brought the same skills to Kipling's *Puck of Pook's Hill*, 1906, and many other books. Other outstanding illustrators in a similar vein were CE Brock—notably with Eleanor Farjeon's lush neo-fairy tales for teenaged girls, *Martin Pippin in the Apple Orchard*, 1921—and his younger brother HM Brock who also illustrated for *The Boy's Own Paper* and *The Captain*; Arthur Hughes, who illustrated for George MacDonald's books, notably *The Princess and the Goblin*, 1871, and Gordon Browne—the son of Dickens' illustrator, 'Phiz' (Hablot K Browne) whose illustrations for SR Crockett's *The Surprising Adventures of Sir Toady Lion*, 1897, reinforced a fashion for books about childhood. In an era when the fairy tale was coming into its own—Andrew Lang's 'Colour Fairy Books', beginning with *The Blue Fairy Book*, 1899, illustrated by Henry J Ford, were hugely popular.

The 'beautiful child' became a popular cult—a sentimental feature of magazines such as *Punch*; Robert Louis Stevenson's *A Child's Garden of Verses*, 1885, was illustrated profusely by Charles Robinson (brother of W Heath Robinson) in 1895. These idealised and stylised children survived from Peter Pan (first performed in 1904) through to AA Milne's *Winnie the Pooh* books in the 1920s—until thoroughly debunked by Richmal Crompton's anti-beautiful-child, William (*Just William*, 1922). The contrast between EH Shepard's gentle and rural depiction of Milne's characters (and his 1931 edition of Kenneth Grahame's *The Wind in the Willows*) and Thomas Henry's depiction of the scruffy and anarchic 'William' points up the contrast.

The beginning of the girls' school story with Angela Brazil's *The Fortunes of Philippa*, 1906, coincided with the descent of the boys' school stories into broad comedy and self-parody. In 1908 the first 'Greyfriars' stories, by the world's most prolific writer, Charles Hamilton (aka Frank Richards and many other pseudonyms) appeared in *The Magnet*.

"Crane borrowed techniques from Japanese printmaking, using flat colouring and sharp outlines."

Lavishly illustrated, these stories were also part of the development of the 'comic'.

The end of the nineteenth century was also a golden age for the picture-book, as colour printing using lithography and early photolithography improved. The modern picture-book is often said to have originated through the work of four illustrators associated with the printer Edmund Evans: Walter Crane, Kate Greenaway, Randolph Caldecott, and Arthur Rackham. Crane borrowed techniques from Japanese printmaking, using flat colouring and sharp outlines, and made extensive use of the 'opening', or double-page spread. His publisher was Frederick Warne, and from 1865 he produced a best-selling series of sixpenny 'toy books', such as *Sing a Song of Sixpence*. Kate Greenaway worked for magazines such as *Little Folks*, and her popularity is demonstrated by the *Kate Greenaway Almanack* produced annually from 1883 to 1895. Although often criticised for the inaccuracy of her drawings of children, she influenced children's fashions then and now and was fond of depicting scenes of an innocent rural world. Her nostalgia for an idealised eighteenth century was shared by Randolph Caldecott in his series of 'toy books', 1878–1886, such as *The Diverting Story of John Gilpin*, 1878. Caldecott enriched his pictures with witty (and apparently inconsequential) detail, a technique still used in the twenty-first century by illustrators such as Helen Craig in her *Angelina* series. There has been a good deal of critical argument as to whether such detail adds richness to the experience of the picture-book, or interferes with the narrative thrust of the books.

The Marquis of Carabas Picture Book, illustrations by Walter Crane, printed in colours by Edmund Evans, courtesy of The Wandsworth Collection.

Arthur Rackham's work, in contrast, is instantly recognisable for its grotesque style; his last work included an edition of *The Wind in the Willows* (completed in 1939) and background paintings for Walt Disney's first full-length cartoon *Snow White and the Seven Dwarfs*, 1936.

Other notable exponents of the colour picture-book at this period were Edmund Dulac from France, Kay Nielsen from Denmark, Willy Pogany from Hungary, and Ida Rentoul Outhwaite from Australia.

Beatrix Potter's *The Tale of Peter Rabbit*, 1902, was one of the first books to use a tri-colour process, with the colour printing-blocks produced using a camera; it was printed by Evans and published by Warne. Potter's intricate water-colours, combining accurate animal-drawing with human characteristics, are deceptively innocent: her tone of voice is ironic, and the world that her characters occupy often dangerous. Very often, her imitators missed the tough-mindedness of the books, but Potter, like Carroll, Kipling, and Nesbit, was instrumental in setting the tone for twentieth century children's books. Frederick Warne's other star artist was L Leslie Brooke, whose most famous book is probably a collection of his own verses, *Johnny Crow's Garden*.

Two remarkable picture-books of the period are still controversial, and both became emblems of racism, even if they were innocent enough at the time: Helen Bannerman's *Little Black Sambo*, 1899, and Florence and Bertha Upton's *The Adventures of Two Dutch Dolls and a Golliwogg*, 1895. (A later book in the Uptons'

series, *The Golliwogg's Auto Go-Cart*, 1902, bears more than a passing resemblance to Toad's adventures in *The Wind in the Willows*.)

There was a parallel flowering of illustration in the United States. The pioneering figure was Howard Pyle—whose work is characterised by pseudo-medievalism. Pyle began his work in the most famous of American children's magazines, *St Nicholas* (from 1873) and his most characteristic book is probably *The Merry Adventures of Robin Hood*, 1883. Among Pyle's pupils were Jessie Wilcox Smith, Maxfield Parrish—who has an immediately-recognisably intricate style of pseudo photo-realism, and NC Wyeth. Wyeth produced spectacular and dramatic paintings for books such as *Treasure Island*, 1911: he worked on large canvasses which were technically difficult to reproduce. WW Denslow illustrated the first edition of *The Wizard of Oz*, 1900, and it was said that the book sold on its illustrations, rather than on its text.

And, of course, the comic was now in full flow. The first comic as we now know it was probably *Funny Folks*, published in 1874; Alfred Harmsworth launched *Comic Cuts* and *Chips* in 1890—both of which survived until 1953. The use of a sequence of frames became increasingly sophisticated, and the comic could aspire to being high art, as with Winsor McCay's *Little Nemo in Slumberland*, 1908.

Left *Johnny Crow's Garden*, illustrations by L Leslie Brooke.
Right *The Story of Little Black Sambo*, by Helen Bannerman, courtesy of The Wandsworth Collection.

The Golliwogg's Auto Go-Cart, Illustrations by Florence Upton,
courtesy of The Wandsworth Collection.

Pooh and beyond

The 1920s and 1930s were remarkable for the number of iconic figures they produced: apart from Pooh Bear, there were Mary Poppins, Biggles, the Hobbit, Dr Seuss, Tarzan, William Brown, Worzel Gummidge, TS Eliot's practical cats, Mickey Mouse and Superman, Desperate Dan and Korky the Cat from *The Dandy*, 1937, and Rupert Bear (by Mary Tourtel from 1920 and by AE Bestall from 1935). Not to mention the main character in the 2.5 million copies of a book given away in 1939 by the Montgomery Ward department store, *Rudolph the Red-Nosed Reindeer*.

Initially, the horrors of the First World War produced a protective and retreatist attitude to childhood, epitomised by AA Milne's *Winnie the Pooh*, 1926, Hugh Lofting's 'Dr Dolittle' series, from 1920 and Arthur Ransome's *Swallows and Amazons*, 1930—the last two both illustrated in 'naïve' style by their authors. Safe, peaceful and domestic village life was celebrated—and illustrated—in Joyce Lankester Brisley's *Milly-Molly-Mandy*, 1928, and Constance Heward's 'Ameliaranne' series, from 1920. Alison Uttley's 'Little Grey Rabbit' series, from 1929, illustrated by Margaret Tempest, produced a rural idyll resembling that of Beatrix Potter, but without her acerbity. The continued lure of this cosy view of the world is demonstrated by the success of Jill Barklem's 'Brambly Hedge' series, 1980 to present. The commercial face of the 'beautiful child' cult can be seen in the work of Mabel Lucie Atwell, who had established herself before the First World War as an illustrator of rubicund toddlers, and who began her long-running *Lucie Atwell's Annual* from 1922. Another survivor from the period is Cicely Mary Barker whose 'Flower Fairy' books, from 1923, are still in print.

This was the hey-day of the girls' school story, for example, Dorita Fairlie Bruce's 'Dimsie' series, from 1920, reflecting solid and safe English values. However, as the 1920s progressed, there was a growing unease and edginess in children's books, reflecting the increasingly unstable situation in continental Europe—*The Girl's Own Paper* was an admirer of the Hitler Youth movement. The 1930s saw the beginning

of the career novel with Noel Streatfeild's *Ballet Shoes*, 1937 with illustrations by her sister, Ruth Gervis, of the sociological novel with Eve Garnett's *The Family from One-end Street*, 1938, with her own pictures, and even of the political novel with Geoffrey Trease's *Bows Against the Barons*, 1934, (later illustrated by C Walter Hodges).

Perhaps the most striking characteristic of the period was the astonishing growth of picture-books, often highly stylised and reflecting contemporary art and design. William Nicholson's *Clever Bill*, 1926, and Edward Ardizzone's *Little Tim and the Brave Sea-Captain*, 1936, are both examples of early photolithography, and both experimented with the word-picture relationship. The influence of continental Europe can be seen in the popularity of the work of the Belgian Hergé (Georges Rémi) who began his hugely

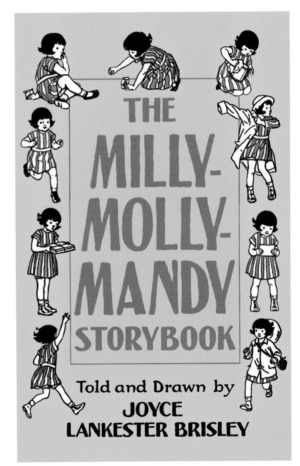

Opposite *Tim to the Rescue*, text and illustrations © Edward Ardizzone 1949. First published by Frances Lincoln 2005.
Above *The Milly Molly Mandy Storybook*, text and illustrations © Joyce Lankester Brisley 1928.

successful 'Tintin' series with a political satire, *Tintin au pays de Soviets* in 1930. The possibilities of the picture-book were extended by Jean de Brunhoff's 'Babar' series, from 1931—in Britain followed by the lush colouring of Kathleen Hale's folio-sized *Orlando the Marmalade Cat*, from 1938. Almost as influential were Walter Trier, who illustrated Erich Kästner's *Emil and the Detectives*, 1929, (Trier moved from Germany to London in 1936), and Jan Lewitt and George Him, who moved to London from Warsaw in 1938, and illustrated Diana Ross' *The Little Red Engine Gets a Name*, 1942.

Less well-remembered, but no less striking books include Arnrid Johnston's *Pigwiggen: His Dashing Career*, 1938, Bernard and Elinor Darwin's *The Tale of Mr Tootleoo*, 1924, Laurian Jones' illustrations for Enid Bagnold's *Alice and Thomas and Jane*, 1930, and Katharine Tozer's philosophical elephant Mumfie, from 1935—whose adventures extended into the Second World War. In *Mumfie Marches On*, 1942, he manages to capture both Hitler and Mussolini.

In the United States, the most famous picture-books were produced by, or influenced by, a wave of European immigrants, such as Miska Petersham, Wanda Gâg (*Millions of Cats*, 1928) and Boris Artzybasheff (*Gay-Neck*, 1927), Ludwig Bemelmans (*Madeline*, 1939), HA Rey (*Curious George*, 1941), and Kurt Weise (*The Story about Ping*, 1933). Other classics in this style included Margery Flack's *Angus and the Ducks*, 1930, and Virginia Lee Burton's two masterpieces, *Mike Mulligan and his Steam Shovel*, 1939, and *The Little House*, 1942, both of which celebrated (and lamented the loss of) an idealised small-town America. A similar semi-political retreatism (especially after the Wall Street crash of 1929), can be found in Laura Ingalls Wilder's 'Little House' books, from 1932, an extended essay on frontier independence, classically illustrated by Garth Williams.

Three slightly eccentric classics might be noted here: Mervyn Peake's surreal *Captain Slaughterboard Drops Anchor*, 1939, the controversially pacifist *The Story of Ferdinand*, 1936, by Munro Leaf, illustrated in a distinctively spare style by Robert Lawson (who went on to win the Newbery medal for the best American picture-book of 1945, *Rabbit Hill*) and Robert McCloskey's city-centre idyll, set in Boston, *Make way for Ducklings*, 1941.

The beginning of the Second World War saw, in England, the beginning of mass-produced picture-books using photolithography—notably Penguin's 'Puffin Picture-books'. Ladybird Books (which had first appeared in 1915) adopted the format that made them into an iconic British series in 1940 with *Bunnikin's Picnic Party* illustrated by AJ MacGregor. The war severely restricted the production of books of any kind—but one author managed to maintain her output. Enid Blyton, who had begun her career in 1922 (and who went on to write over 600 books) was one of the few authors whose paper-allowance was not reduced. She produced 86 books between 1939 and 1945, including the first 'Famous Five' books (*Five on a Treasure Island*, 1942), and the 'Mary Mouse' books, illustrated by Olive F Openshaw, from 1942, which were printed on paper off-cuts. Of her many illustrators, Eileen Soper became closely identified with her work, while Stuart Tresilian produced some distinguished illustrations for the up-market *The Island of Adventure*, 1944 and its sequels. Blyton is particularly significant in the history of children's books and illustration, in that she exercised tight control over the choice of illustrator, the pictures they produced, and the overall design of her books. For the 'Noddy' books, 1949 to present, illustrated by Harmsen van der Beek, which established a new standard for brightly coloured picture-books, she was instrumental in designing a uniform 'brand' image—pioneering the skillful commodification of children's literature that was to follow.

The Story of Barbar, by Jean de Brunhoff, first published 1931.

Illustrators and Authors 1659–1945

Just look at him! There he stands,
With his nasty hair and hands.
See! his nails are never cut;
They are grim'd as black as soot;
And the sloven, I declare,
Never once has comb'd his hair;
Any thing to me is sweeter
Than to see Shock-headed Peter.

Alice's Adventures in Wonderland
Lewis Carroll

Alice's Adventures in Wonderland is regarded as a liberating work within the history of children's literature. It marked the start of a change from books with heavy underlying moral values, to books which appealed to children's imaginations, existing to entertain and excite them, and has influenced subsequent children's writers ever since.

Its author, Lewis Carroll, had two very contrasting sides to his character. Under his real name, Charles Lutwidge Dodgson, he worked as a mathematician at Christchurch college; yet he also possessed a wild, child-like imagination which allowed him to produce his celebrated work of literary 'nonsense' and expose the world to his surreal wonderland. Carroll wrote a sequel to Alice entitled _Through the Looking Glass_, the narrative of which is often thought to have been a part of the original title, and other work such as _Sylvie and Bruno_, which is similar in style to the Alice titles. It has been said that he never truly outgrew his childhood, and felt more at ease with children than he did with adults. He struck up a friendship with ten year old Alice Liddell, daughter of the Dean of Christchurch, and whilst out for a boat trip

with her and her sisters, he began telling a story which later developed into _Alice's Adventures in Wonderland_. Carroll illustrated a version of the story himself that he presented to Alice Liddell as a gift.

Alice herself has become a phenomena, a character who is recognisable even to people who have not read the book. She was the first heroine to be a young girl who has the capability to tell her story from her own perspective. It is she who is the unifying power in the story, bringing all the nonsense together; a lone child voice of rationality in a world of adult madness.

The original illustrations were produced by John Tenniel, a largely self taught artist who studied for a period at the Royal Academy before working as a cartoonist for _Punch_ magazine. When he came to work on _Alice's Adventures in Wonderland_ he was able to fuse his earlier archaic and refined work with his developed _Punch_ drawing style to create fresh and highly individual images.

Opposite bottom and this page *Alice's Adventures in Wonderland*, illustrations by John Tenniel.
Opposite top *Alice's Adventures Underground*, being a facsimile of the 1886 original, illustrations by the author.

The illustrations for *Alice* were produced using an early printing process called xylography. The original printing blocks are now held in the Bodleian Library in Oxford, though are seldom exhibited. Tenniel had objections over the print quality of the first two thousand editions, which he voiced to Carroll. Carroll insisted that the books be recalled and reprinted, demonstrating his respect for Tenniel and his work on *Alice*.

After Tenniel, one of the most loved *Alice* illustrators is Arthur Rackham, whose edition was published in 1907 after the death of Carroll and when the novel became free of copyright in the UK. Alice in Rackham's illustrations is beautifully drawn and realistically portrayed yet the world of Wonderland around her is ominous and unsettling, the characters strange and misshapen.

Above *Alice's Adventures in Wonderland*, illustrations by Arthur Rackham, © care of the Bridgeman Art Library/The Estate of Arthur Rackham.
Opposite Illustration © 1988 Anthony Browne. From *Alice's Adventures in Wonderland* by Lewis Carroll and illustrated by Anthony Browne.
Reproduced by permission of Walker Books Ltd, London SE11 5HJ.

Alice's Adventures in Wonderland has been re-imagined by many esteemed artists, writers and illustrators. Amongst these are Surrealist master Salvador Dali, whose portfolio on *Alice* features a signature melting clock as the table at the Hatter's Tea Party, and Ralph Steadman, whose version of the famous "drink me" bottle is designed as a Coca Cola bottle.

Further popular illustrators who have recreated their own vision of Wonderland include Helen Oxenbury, Michael Foreman, Anthony Bowne and a pop-up version by Robert Sabuda.

Beyond these there has been a television series, song lyrics, music videos, animations and a number of films, the most recent a re-imagining by Tim Burton. It seems the journey through the rabbit hole will continue for years to come.

Below *Alice's Adventures in Wonderland*, © 2003 Robert Sabuda, Published by Simon and Schuster in 2003.
Opposite Illustrations © 2005 Helen Oxenbury, from *Alice Through the Looking Glass*, written by Lewis Carroll and illustrated by Helen Oxenbury. Reproduced by permission of Walker Books Ltd, London SE11 5HJ.

Edward Ardizzone

Despite being born in Vietnam and having an Itallian surname, Edward Ardizzone encapsulates the respected tradition of great English illustration, and kept that tradition alive throughout the twentieth century.

His distinctive, atmospheric drawings continue to delight children and his basic fusion of the everyday and the exotic make for a truly enjoyable read.

His work was rooted in the great watercolour style of esteemed artists of the eighteenth and nineteenth centuries such as Cruikshank, Rowlandson and Caldecott. His delicate yet fluent illustrations lent themselves to children's books perfectly, and the ease with which he transformed text into image and movement gave an atmospheric vitality to every story he worked on.

Ardizzone was always influenced by what was happening around him, and a great deal of his work recreated the times he spent living in Maida Vale, where he developed his cross-hatched, vigorous yet smooth style. Some of his best-loved books include the *Tim* series, which he wrote for his son Phillip, and were partly realised from experiences of Ardizzone's own childhood. Tim lived by the docks where the sea would frequently call him out to danger and adventure. The books played on stereotypical Victorian pokerfaced affectations, and the illustrations were inter-cut with dry witticisms from the characters.

From *Tim to the Rescue* to *Tim in Danger*, the books were celebrated for their balance, pacing and pinpoint timing of both the text and the illustrations, all key ingredients for a great picture-book.

Ardizzone used many different techniques in his work including watercolour, oil and printing methods, but the majority of his picture-books were produced with a line and wash method, giving his illustrations a spontaneous feel although they were actually re-worked and perfected many times until Ardizzone was completely satisfied. He drew constantly in sketchbooks or anything else available and had a great ability to recreate the world around him. During his career Ardizzone illustrated over 180 books, including work accompanying Shakespeare, Dickens and Water de la Mare. His own stories are known for their simple text and the importance of a sudden turning point in the narrative, such as in *Johnny the Clockmaker* when self-styled handyman Johnny attempts to build a grandfather clock, against the advice of his parents and friends. Johnny's saviour is his friend Susannah, and despite the odds, together they do manage to finish the clock; the story's message being that anything is possible. The ease with which Ardizzone's illustrations can be understood and appreciated made him a master storyteller, producing a wordless book, in *Johnny's Bad Day*.

Left *Tim to the Rescue*, text and illustrations © Edward Ardizzone 1949. First published by Francis Lincoln 2005.
Opposite Original artwork, courtesy of the Seven Stories Collection, from *Tim in Danger*, text and illustrations © Edward Ardizzone 1953. First published Francis Lincoln 2006.

TIM IN DANGER

by
Edward Ardizzone

Oxford University Press
London   New York   Toronto

Tim and Charlotte's best friend on board was the second mate. He was a very fat man and a very sad one too. He was sad because he was always unlucky and felt that nobody liked him. He was, however, a kind man and would often say 'Now children, stop work and sit down and talk to me.'

Then they would tell him about their home by the sea and about Tim's mother and father and Ginger. He would sigh and say that he wished he had a nice home like other people.

To tell you the truth he was really very unlucky. Everything he did went wrong. The captain would get terribly cross with him and

For the first few days Charlotte found the work very hard and when she was alone in her bunk she could not help crying a little and wishing she was at home. But, as she was a very good cook, she soon became a great favourite with the crew.

Tim found the work hard too and was often very bored with scrubbing and cleaning. However, as he always tried to do his best and never complained, everybody was very nice to him.

Opposite and above Original artwork, courtesy of the Seven Stories Collection, from *Tim in Danger*, text and illustrations © Edward Ardizzone 1953. First published Francis Lincoln 2006.

Johnny the Clockmaker, text and illustrations © Edward Ardizzone 1960.
First published Francis Lincoln 2008.

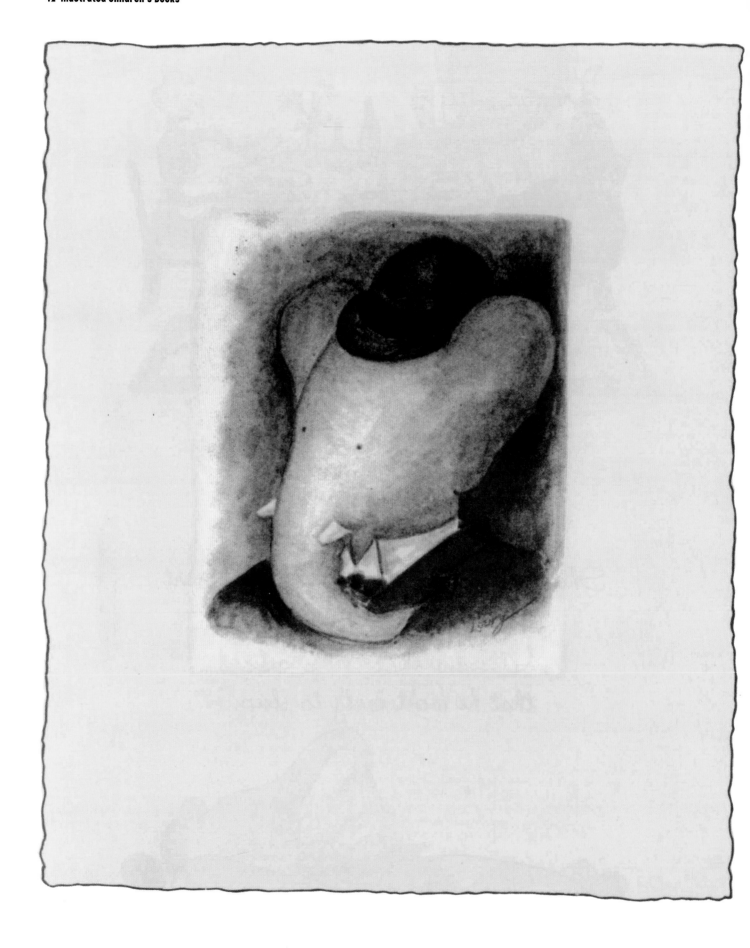

Babar
Jean de Brunhoff

Perhaps the only aristocratic elephant existing in children's literature, Babar first trumpeted into picture-books in 1931. Upon its release, *Histoire de Babar* (*The Story of Babar*) by Jean de Brunhoff, was an instant success; its oversized pages, colourful lithographed drawings and handwritten text made Babar a highly original hit in its time.

Histoire de Babar begins with one of the most brutal beginnings of picture-books; Babar's mother is shot dead by a faceless hunter. Babar runs off to fend for himself, and there is little time to recover from this sudden turn of events. The book has been criticised for its insensitive response to the trauma, and throughout the series the wound is never treated or healed.

Babar wanders into a city that seems to encapsulate Paris, but is also presumably an amalgamation of various French colonial cities along the North African coast. He revels in its bourgeois delights, and finds himself easily adjusting to the human way of life. However, it is not long before he begins to miss his savannah, and so returns to his elephant existence. On his return, the other elephants marvel at his acquired human characteristics and make him "King of the Elephants". Babar sets about turning the savannah into his own mini-Paris, and it is this link or tension between the savannah and the city that forms the structure for the whole series.

Despite Babar's success he has also been described as an allegory of French colonialism, and Jean de Brunhoff accused of creating imperialist propaganda. Babar is attracted by the power of civilisation, and easily assimilated into a bourgeois lifestyle, which he then imposes on the other 'inferior' elephants. Although this is viewed by some as a malicious expression of colonialism, the Babar series is a deliberate play on typical aristocratic and imperialist attitudes relating to the French imagination and harks back to a nostalgic view of pre-1914 France.

Jean de Brunhoff only completed six Babar stories in his lifetime, but the Babar helm was taken up by his son Laurent, who has stretched the series over 30 subsequent books.

All illustrations from *The Story of Babar* by Jean de Brunhoff. First published 1931.

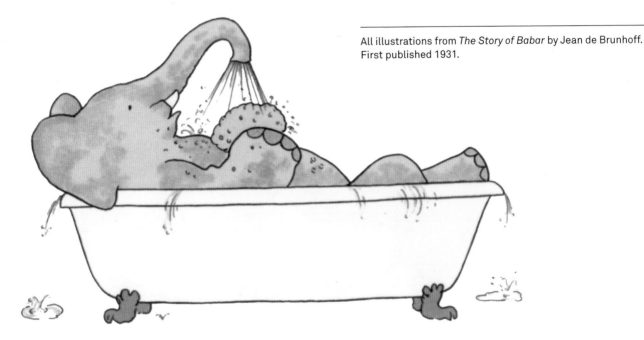

Like all little boys, Arthur and Zephir
were always up to mischief;
but they were not lazy.
At the Old Lady's house, Babar and Celeste
were astonished to hear them playing
the violin and 'cello.
"It's wonderful!" cried Celeste, and Babar said:
"Children, I am pleased with you.
Go to the cake-shop and choose whatever you like."

The Story of Little Black Sambo by Helen Bannerman.
All images courtesy of The Wandsworth Collection.

Helen Bannerman

Scottish author and illustrator Helen Bannerman lived a large part of her life in India. Influenced by her time there, many of the heroes in her books are recognisably South Indian or Tamil, the most famous of which is *Little Black Sambo*.

Written in 1898, the book tells the story of a young boy, Sambo, who puts on his finest new clothes to take a walk in the jungle. He encounters tigers on his walk and, one by one, is forced to give them items of his clothing to stop them from eating him. Sambo is devastated to have lost all his beautiful clothing, until he hears the tigers growling and fighting over who looks the grandest. Sambo sneaks up and reclaims his clothes, whilst the tigers chase each other around a tree so fast that they turn into butter, which Sambo and his family eat with pancakes for dinner.

Over the years the book has become surrounded by controversy and accused of reflecting white supremacist attitudes and perpetuating racist stereotypes. However, some readers, especially those in America, would have not learned the story from Bannerman's original illustrations, but from many of the reprinted and cheaper editions which featured grotesque, degrading caricatures.

Little Black Sambo himself is a courageous and feisty hero who outwits the tigers, and his inventiveness is celebrated in the book. The final image of Sambo and his parents enjoying eating the melted tiger butter is darkly comic, and perhaps harks back to Bannerman's Scottish roots.

Thomas Bewick

Thomas Bewick was a celebrated English wood engraver, who developed a sophisticated technique, with fine lines, tones and textures, and subtle contrast, which took wood engraving to new heights in the late eighteenth century.

Wood engraving at the time had more typically been relegated to the production of simple woodcuts for chapbooks, but Bewick was able to print with more precision by using harder woods and finer tools normally used by metal engravers.

Newcastle-born, Bewick went to work for local engraving firm Beilby, where wood engraving was only a small proportion of the business. Nonetheless, here he developed the skills that he began to combine with his love of drawing nature—particularly animals. In 1790, he published *A General History of Quadrupeds*, a highly popular educational book about mammals from around the world, aimed at children as well as adults. He followed this with two volumes of *A History of British Birds* (*Land Birds* 1797, and *Water Birds* 1804). The first book inevitably contained illustrations of some non-British animals that it is unlikely that he drew from life; the birds in the second two volumes were more likely to have been drawn from nature.

Part of the popularity of these books was Bewick's inclusion of small scenes at the end of selected sections, which he called 'tale-pieces'. These vignettes appeared throughout the book, and offered a supplementary story to the book's main narrative. Bewick's tale-pieces were made using the end-grain of blocks of box-wood, which resulted in a very fine line. As an engraver he worked with a team of apprentices, some of whom went on to become distinguished engravers themselves such as William Harvey and Bewick's own son, Robert Elliott Bewick.

Although these two major works are probably his best known, Bewick was a prolific artist, producing a number of illustrations for children's book, such as a new edition of *Aesop's Fables*. Bewick and his apprentice's illustrations brought to life in ways more precise than ever before the memorable moments from Aesop's classic tales, and although Bewick himself described the process as pleasurable yet arduous, they remain a beautiful accompaniment to the classic tales.

Above *A General History of Quadrupeds*.
Courtesy of the Natural History Society of Northumbria.
Right *A History of British Birds, Volume I (Land Birds)*.
Courtesy of the Natural History Society of Northumbria.
Opposite *Fables* by Walter Brown, with cuts by Thomas Bewick.
Courtesy of The Wandsworth Collection.

L Leslie Brooke

L (Leonard) Leslie Brooke is a British author and illustrator, best known for the *Johnny Crow* books, which began in 1903 with *Johnny Crow's Garden*, a beautifully illustrated series of his own playful rhymes.

He began work as an illustrator in his late 20s, working on stories by Evelyn Everett-Green, a British writer of stories for girls. His drawings for Andrew Lang's *Nursery Rhyme Book* in 1889 established him as a leading illustrator; these were followed by work including an edition of Edward Lear poems, *The Pelican Chorus*, c.1899, and *The Jumblies and Other Nonsense Verses*, 1900, for which his quiet sense of the absurd was particularly appropriate. He illustrated many classic nursery rhymes; however, it was the *Johnny Crow* books that established him as a major British figure.

An admirer of Randolph Caldecott, Brooke's style is characterised by high-quality draftsmanship skills, combined with a talent for wit and humour.

Left *Johnny Crow's Gardens*, illustrations by L Leslie Brooke.
Right *Oranges and Lemons*, illustrations by L Leslie Brooke.

Top *Oranges and Lemons*, illustrations by L Leslie Brooke.
Bottom *Little Bo-Beep*, illustrations by L Leslie Brooke.

Above and opposite *The Butterfly's Ball and the Grasshopper's Feast,* illustrated by William Mulready.
All images courtesy of The Wandsworth Collection.

The Butterfly's Ball and the Grasshopper's Feast
William Roscoe

The Butterfly's Ball and the Grasshopper's Feast was a children's poem, popular in England from its first publication in *Gentlemens' Magazine* in 1806.

The poem tells the story of the night a party was held for a host of insects and other creatures—including a beetle, gnat and an ant, a dormouse, frog and a squirrel—who eat and dance under light provided by a glow-worm.

London bookseller and children's book publisher John Harris first produced the poem as a separate publication in January 1807. The text is attributed to William Roscoe, MP for Liverpool at the time, and the first edition illustrations were copperplates after drawings by William Mulready.

The story is itself highly visual, lending itself well to illustration. Many different editions by different publishers appeared over the next few decades. The story has also been published in the United States, and as a chapbook. Through the various editions, the creatures and insects have been represented more or less realistically, often with anthropomorphic qualities.

Over 150 years later, in 1973, British artist and illustrator Alan Aldridge produced an award-winning (Whitbread Children's Book of the Year, 1973) picture-book based on the poem, with revised text by William Plomer (novelist and poet); he then turned this into an animation in 1974, with a song, "Love is All" written by Roger Glover, bassist and song writer for Deep Purple. Glover turned it into a concept album in 1974 and rock opera in 1975.

**" Come take up your Hats, and away let us haste
To the Butterfly's Ball, and the Grasshopper's Feast.
The Trumpeter, Gad-fly, has summon'd the Crew,
And the Revels are now only waiting for you. "**

Randolph Caldecott

Randolph Caldecott is one of the major British illustrators of the late eighteenth century, best known for the set of children's picture-books that he produced with pioneering colour printer Edmund Evans; each Christmas from 1878 to 1886, the pair produced two new books together, priced at one shilling. They were an instant hit.

Caldecott would choose a nursery rhyme, a piece of contemporary verse or nonsense for the text he would then illustrate, in colour or black and white. His style was not dissimilar to Greenaway's or Crane's, who also worked with Edmund Evans, though his drawing style is typically seen as looser, and the scenes he draws wittier; together the three set the tone for children's illustrations in the late eighteenth century.

In 1883, he produced his own illustrated version of images in *Aesop's Fables: Some of Aesop's Fables with Modern Instances Shewn in Designs by Randolph Caldecott*. The 20 fables include "The Man and his two wives", "The Fox without a Tail" and "The Frogs Desiring a King". Each fable was illustrated in black and white across a double page spread; in each case, on the left hand side, the fable would be illustrated as a simple narrative while, on the right hand side, the 'modern instance' is a cartoon that re-tells the fable in a contemporary context.

Not only was Caldecott commercially successful, his work was also highly influential. Admirers include Beatrix Potter, L Leslie Brooke (*Johnny Crow's Garden*, 1903) and Maurice Sendak (*Where the Wild Things Are*, 1963) while, since 1938, the annual Caldecott Medal has been awarded in the United States to the best American children's picture-book.

Above and opposite top *An Elegy on the Death of a Mad Dog*, by Oliver Goldsmith, illustrations by Randolph Caldecott.
Opposite bottom *Hey Diddle Diddle and Baby Bunting, Randolph Caldecott's Picture Books*.
All images courtesy of The Wandsworth Collection.

**" In Islington there lived a man,
Of whom the world might say,
That still a godly race he ran.... "**

Chapbooks

These cheap pocket-sized booklets or pamphlets, usually illustrated with simple woodcuts, told stories and popular tales, and were sold by travelling pedlars or 'chapmen' in Britain from the sixteenth to the nineteenth century, though they were seen in other countries too. Titles such as *The Renowned History of Dame Trot and her Cat* were favourites in America.

As well as a form of popular fiction, chapbooks provided an ideal educational tool, or a vehicle for spreading sometimes controversial political thought, because of the sheer quantity that could be produced and distributed.

Chapbooks were typically printed on a single, folded sheet of paper and, as a result, could contain between eight and 24 pages. The quality of the writing, images, and production varied. Some were stitched, some bound, others were given a simple cover. The type size would sometimes be made larger or smaller in order to fill the space, and crude woodcuts illustrated the stories, though the best quality chapbooks contained well-written stories and more sophisticated woodcuts.

Compared to books, chapbooks were cheap to produce and cheap to buy; they provided relatively easily accessible stories for those who otherwise would have had limited access to literature, particularly those in rural areas and helped to develop literacy in these areas. Other forms of popular literature eventually took over the role of the chapbook, including cheaper newspapers.

The many tales included *Cinderella*, *Little Red Riding Hood*, *Tom Thumb*, *Jack the Giant Killer* and more political offerings such as *The Tichbourne Trial*. Over time, the material presented began to include well-known nursery rhymes including *Jack and Jill*, *Jack Sprat* and *Tom the Piper's Son*.

> " This is the Cabman,
> who first brought
> In his brand new cab
> the claimant to court,
> The man like his cab
> has now grown old,
> And the horse that drew
> it was long since sold.
> And scores since then
> that cab that drew, Have
> gone to the knackers
> for aught I know. "

Opposite *Cinderella.*
Top *The Tichborne Trial, As Told to Our Grandchildren.*
Bottom right *The Renowned History of Dame Trot and her Cat.*
Bottom left *The History of Tom Thumb.*
All images courtesy of The Wandsworth Collection.

Walter Crane

A part of the Arts and Crafts Movement in Britain in the late nineteenth and early twentieth centuries, Walter Crane was an English artist and book illustrator whose work ranged from painting to wallpaper design, book illustration to textiles.

Crane enjoyed a long and fruitful relationship with Edmund Evans, a printer who was instrumental in the development of the children's illustrated book, and who was in part responsible for the popularity of the books by the great English illustrators of that period: Crane, Kate Greenaway and Randolph Caldecott. From about 1865, Crane produced in the region of 50 children's picture-books for Evans, generally around traditional stories or fairy tales, such as *Bluebeard*, *The Marquis of Carabas* and *Puss in Boots*.

The influence of the Pre-Raphaelites is clear in Crane's work, which is elegantly and minutely detailed. His work in window design also translated into his picture-book illustrations. They sometimes channelled a stained glass window aesthetic, particularly in their colour schemes, which often featured glowing reds and oranges, broken

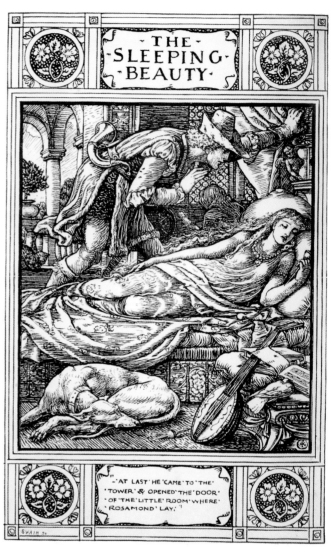

Left *The Baby's Own Aesop. Being the fables condensed in rhyme with portable morals pictorially pointed by Walter Crane.*
Above *Brothers Grimm*, translated from the German by Lucy Crane, with pictures by Walter Crane.
Opposite *The Blue Beard Picture Book. Containing Blue Beard, Little Red Riding Hood, Jack and the Bean-stalk, The Sleeping Beauty.* With 32 pages of illustrations by Walter Crane.
All images courtesy of The Wandsworth Collection.

BLUEBEARD.

ONCE on a time there lived a man
    hated by all he knew,
Both that his ways were very bad,
    and that his beard was blue;
But as he was so rich and grand, and
    led a merry life,
A lady he contrived at last to induce
    to be his wife.

Out set Riding Hood, so obliging and
sweet,
And she met a great Wolf in the wood,
Who began most politely the maiden to
greet,
In as tender a voice as he could.

He asked to what house she was going,
and why;
Red Riding Hood answered him all:
He said, "Give my love to your Gran; I
will try
"At my earliest leisure to call."

up by bold blues. Other projects explored by Crane included working as a cartoonist for Socialist papers *Justice* and *The Commonwealth*. He became involved with the Socialist movement of the 1880s through his friend the designer William Morris, and they both strived to introduce art to the daily lives of all classes.

Despite other ventures, illustrated children's books were an ideal medium for Crane's style and technique. He was not skilled at drawing from life, but had a talent for working with a flattened image, also evident in his wallpaper and textile designs. In his work with Evans, he showed an understanding of the possibilities of colour printing. He typically used the full frame of the picture, developed a rich use of colour and bold black outline, and had a careful eye for detail. Crane showed from his earliest work an interest in the unity of text and image and was keen to integrate the two together, as he did for *Lady of Shalott*, where he printed the poem with his own calligraphy.

Crane's work accompanying nursery rhymes and fairy tales such as *Bluebeard*, *Hey Diddle Diddle* and his wonderfully gothic *Grimm's Fairy Tales* proved hugely influential, and his innocent, joyful 'child-in-the-garden' motifs set the tone for popular children's illustration for years to come.

Opposite *The Blue Beard Picture Book*, "Little Red Riding Hood".
Above *The Baby's Own Aesop*.
All images courtesy of The Wandsworth Collection.

Kate Greenaway

British artist, writer and illustrator, Kate Greenaway presented a beautiful, idealised view of the English countryside, and an innocent and romanticised childhood.

In *Under the Window*, her first published work, a series of her drawings accompanied her own verse. Edmund Evans, celebrated printer of children's books in colour, who acted as 'patron' to Greenaway, as well as to Walter Crane and Randolph Caldecott, saw the appeal of the quaint nature of both her images and verse.

Published by George Routledge & Sons, Evans printed the book beautifully. As a result, at six shillings, it was expensive to buy (relative to the more usual sixpenny and shilling books available at the time). Competitors thought that he would lose money, but the book was a success; published for Christmas 1879, 20,000 copies of the first edition were printed; reprints brought the total printed in English alone to 70,000.

Above *Marigold Garden*, by Kate Greenaway, courtesy of The Wandsworth Collection.
Opposite Illustration by Kate Greenaway from the 1886–1887 volume of *Girl's Own Annual*, courtesy Moira Allen.

Kate Greenaway went on to produce many more titles, including *A Apple Pie*, 1886, *The Language of Flowers*, 1884, and *Marigold Garden*, 1885.

Kate Greenaway's nostalgic depiction of an almost imaginary world reflects her romanticised memory of her own childhood—though she was born in Hoxton, East London, she spent most of her childhood in rural Nottinghamshire. Even her early work shows evidence of her later style—children in the semi-fictitious eighteenth century clothing that inspired a fashion for 'Kate Greenaway' clothes. Her imagery enjoys perennial popularity, with her most celebrated works still in print.

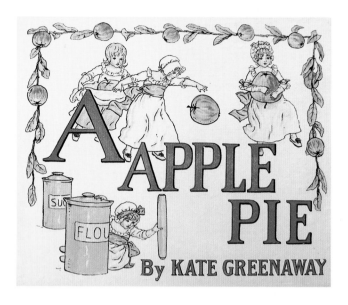

Opposite *A Apple Pie*, by Kate Greenaway, courtesy of
The Wandsworth Collection.
Above *Marigold Garden*, by Kate Greenaway, courtesy of
The Wandsworth Collection.

The Jungle Book and Just So Stories
Rudyard Kipling

Famous for his representations of colonial Britain as much as for his children's books, Rudyard Kipling is often remembered as being first and foremost "the Poet of the British Empire and its yeoman (common solider)".

Born in Bombay but educated in England, Kipling returned to India in 1882 as a young man. He worked as a journalist and editor and began to write about his experiences in India and his views on the Anglo Indian rule over it; these themes would remain key throughout his work. His first works of poetry were published in 1886, and demonstrate Kipling's preoccupations with the soldier and the way of life in societies different from his own.

Between 1893 and 1894 Kipling's famous *The Jungle Book* series began to be published in magazines as a collection of short stories. The anthropomorphic animals in the stories help Mowgli, a human child raised by wolves, and provide moral lessons on courage, honour, integrity and other such noble qualities. Kipling poured into the books all he knew or had been told about the jungle and his "Laws of the Jungle" laid down rules that could be transferred into the human world. The first edition contained some illustrations by Kipling's father, John Lockwood Kipling, and Kipling himself also provided illustrations. *The Jungle Book* has remained a childrens classic and inspired many new illustrated versions, such as Michael Foreman's in 1987 and Robert Ingpen's in 2007.

Other popular children's works by Kipling include the *Just So Stories* published in 1902, which tell fantastic versions of the origins of animal's forms and appearances. A precursor to the tales appears in *The Second Jungle Book*, where Mowgli learns how the tiger got his stripes. The stories were originally illustrated by Kipling, and he depicts the animals in faraway lands with typically strong blocks of black contrasted with light sketches and white space to detail the various stories.

Although Kipling has been accused of colonial prejudices and a glamourisation of militarism, some judge the examples of his work that strongly represent these views as ironic. He was awarded the Nobel Prize for Literature in 1907, making him the first English language recipient and to this day its youngest. Although Kipling will be remembered for a range of work and contributions to English literature, his pioneering of the short story and picture-book will remain amongst his greatest triumphs.

Opposite Illustration from *Just So Stories* © 1987 Michael Foreman, reproduced by permission of the artist.
Below *Just So Stories for Little Children*, original illustrations by Rudyard Kipling. Courtesy of The Wandsworth Collection.

Edward Lear

Edward Lear is best known for his love of the nonsensical in his witty poetry. His pioneering of the nonsense verse along with his humorous illustrations were welcomed as a breath of fresh air from the typically rigid and strict attitudes of the Victorian age within which he lived.

An accomplished fine artist, Lear's early ambition was to become a landscape painter. However, brought up by his sister as a result of failing family fortunes, financial pressure moved him towards the more commercially viable field of illustration very early in his career.

Lear would often visit London Zoo to sketch the parrots, and his first publication *Illustrations of the Family of Psittacidae*, or *Parrots* as it was also known, was accepted when he was just 19. Throughout his life Lear frequently drew birds into his illustrations, or featured them in his poetry.

The collection of limericks in *A Book of Nonsense*, 1846, was highly influential and cemented Lear's reputation as a poet and illustrator, as well as helping to popularise the limerick. His poems were characterised by their use of wordplay, the presence of colour and the physicality of his characters, all of which would often be a key element in his absurd narratives.

The main characters of his poems were often likeable rule-breakers, who were juxtaposed with the presence of a pompous, disagreeable mass, always referred to as "they". The drawings accompanying his poems showed rounded, out of proportion characters with protruding bellies and stumpy legs often portrayed in mid-movement, and such illustrations can be likened to caricature. However, he seemingly disliked feeling obligated to a traditional narrative, and many of his works are completely devoid of an obvious point or basis in reality. He would invent his own words and phrases, such as the "runcible spoon" mentioned at the end of his famous poem *The Owl and the Pussycat*. Although his works are remembered for their light heartedness and humour, Lear himself was victim to periods of depression, which he referred to as "The Morbids". He suffered from epilepsy, but some attitudes of the time believed the disease to be evidence of demonism, and Lear hid his condition in his private life and from the public. His idiosyncratic and original style show him to be a man who could observe the world around him, and seemingly make light of himself, while at the same time secretly struggling against a melancholy which shadowed much of his life.

A Book of Nonsense by Edward Lear.
All images courtesy of The Wandsworth Collection.

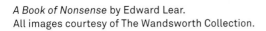

A

BOOK OF NONSENSE.

BY EDWARD LEAR.

Madeline
Ludwig Bemelmans

Ludwig Bemelmans' child-like, innately innocent *Madeline* stories capture both the magic of a spirited child and the beauty of Paris. Madeline is the smallest yet feistiest of 12 girls in her Parisian boarding school, and the series follows her adventures around the city.

Bemelmans uses his impressionist style to represent the world from the eyes of a child, highlighting aspects of it that adults would not notice and using minimal text in rhyming couplets to recount brave Madeline's stories.

Madeline herself is a bold and lovable heroine, who has spawned her own television show and film, as well as continued books, now written by Bemelmans' grandson John Bemelmans Marciano. An internationally recognised figure of mischief and good heart, the original *Madeline* title introduces us to the little girl who would become a huge phenomenon.

Depicting Madeline's daily life in her boarding school with Miss Clavel and her 11 friends, the equilibrium is disrupted when Miss Clavel wakes suddenly in the night, convinced that "Something is not right!" The something is Madeline's appendix, and she is rushed to hospital to have it fixed. Madeline's influence is clear when the other girls cry all night after paying her a visit: "Boohoo, we want to have our appendix out too!"

The book's setting in the boarding school and the archaic charm of 12 little girls parading around in their matching boater hats, set against the beauty of pre-Second World War Paris, mark it as a part of its time which can still be enjoyed by modern readers. The Scholastic edition begins with a list of Parisian landmarks that feature in the book, "for those who may wish to identify the Paris scenes". Although the story is innately linked to Paris and French Catholic traditions, it has generated a huge following from readers across the world.

Bemelmans himself was born in Austria to Belgian and German parents but moved to America when he was a young man. He was made an American citizen in 1918 and his links to different nationalities perhaps help to explain Madeline's wide appeal in both America and Europe. In Bemelmans' last offering, *Madeline in America and Other Holiday Tales*, she actually travels to America to visit her great-grandfather. Bemelmans produced six Madeline titles in total. With John Bemelmans Marciano continuing his grandfather's work, the most recent title is *Madeline and the Cats of Rome*, published in 2008.

" To the tiger in the zoo Madeline just said, "Pooh-pooh",

and nobody knew so well how to frighten Miss Clavel. "

Struwwelpeter
Heinrich Hoffmann

***Struwwelpeter* (Shock Headed Peter) is a gruesome series of moral tales where bad behaviour is punished with bizarre and over exaggerated consequences, and includes 24 pages of full colour illustrations.**

The book's author, Heinrich Hoffmann, wanted to buy his three-year-old son a book for Christmas, but was so unimpressed by the material he found that he decided to buy a notebook and write one himself. His friends later convinced him to publish it, and *Struwwelpeter* became a huge hit with readers across Europe.

The stories have been criticised for being overly violent and gruesome, for example "The Dreadful Story about Harriet and the Matches" where a young pyrotechnic ignores the advice of her mother to leave the matches alone, and consequently is reduced to a pile of ashes on the floor; or "The Story of Little Suck-a Thumb", who has both his thumbs snipped off by a travelling tailor.

This raises the question of whether the stories are cruel and sadistic or humorously entertaining. Although the violence depicted is undoubtedly harsh, it is in some ways no different than the violence that children experience everyday in watching contemporary cartoons or playing computer games.

At the time of first publication (1844), *Struwwelpeter's* humorous text was appreciated by adults, and the imbedded moral values layered amongst the rhyming couplets offered cautionary 'lessons in life' to the child readers.

The bright but slightly off kilter illustrations are absurd and amusing yet at the same time carry a dark foreboding which lies in the subtext of the book. Despite the somewhat sinister qualities, the book's original title of *Funny Stories and Droll Pictures* indicate that Hoffmann intended, at least partly, to entertain as much as to scare.

There are various theories as to how Hoffmann originated the idea, but one possibility lies in the fact that "struwwelpeter" was a word used in Frankfurt to describe those who had become mixed up in revolutionary movements, inviting trouble and personal risk.

The cautionary tales all carry a stark message, a warning, which may reflect Hoffmann's own liberal leanings, mingled with his talent for satire and comedy.

The stories are now regarded as a landmark in the history of children's literature. They have been reprinted and reinterpreted many times. From appearances in DC comics, references in *Charlie and the Chocolate Factory* and new editions by Mark Twain, *Struwwelpeter* has also been re-produced in a musical co-directed by Julian Bleach. It is clear that Shock Headed Peter, alongside the book's other bizarre characters, have stood the test of time.

The English Struwwelpeter or Pretty Stories and Funny Pictures by Heinrich Hoffmann.
All images courtesy of The Wandsworth Collection.

Treasure Island
Robert Louis Stevenson

Robert Louis Stevenson's *Treasure Island* is one of the great classics of children's literature. Written in 1881, it was first released in *Young Folks* magazine as a series of tales under the original title *The Sea Cook*. Stevenson revised the text and changed the title for the 1883 book release, and *Treasure Island* was an instant success. The great story of adventure and acute study of man's behaviour continues to thrill readers to this day.

Stevenson himself was a great traveller, but after journeying to Southern climates, he was forced to return to his native Scotland to try and improve his health as he was suffering from tuberculosis. Whilst in recovery, Stevenson watched his stepson draw out a map of an island; Stevenson joined in and elaborated on the drawing, and gave the map a name, "Skeleton Island". Within three days of drawing the map, Stevenson had written the first three chapters for a story that, of course, became *Treasure Island*.

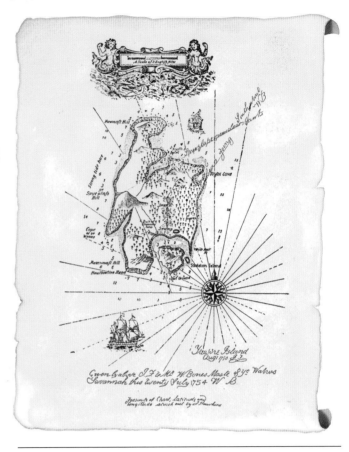

Opposite "One more step, Mr. Hands," said I, "and I'll blow your brains out", an illustration from *Treasure Island* by Robert Louis Stevenson, published by Charles Scribner's Sons, 1911, with colour lithography by Wyeth, Newell Convers, 1882–1945. Private Collection/ The Stapleton Collection/The Bridgeman Art Library.
Left and above Illustrations © 2009 Michael Foreman, from *Treasure Island*, reproduced by permission of Pavilion Children's Books an imprint of Anova Books Ltd.

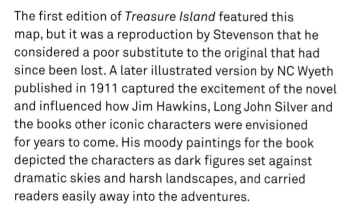

The first edition of *Treasure Island* featured this map, but it was a reproduction by Stevenson that he considered a poor substitute to the original that had since been lost. A later illustrated version by NC Wyeth published in 1911 captured the excitement of the novel and influenced how Jim Hawkins, Long John Silver and the books other iconic characters were envisioned for years to come. His moody paintings for the book depicted the characters as dark figures set against dramatic skies and harsh landscapes, and carried readers easily away into the adventures.

Illustrator Michael Foreman also lent his talents to *Treasure Island*, and his love of all tones of blue work harmoniously with the great tale of adventure. Stormy seas and setting skies painted skilfully in watercolour bring the story to life once again for new generations of readers who desire to sail away with the classic pirate adventure.

Left and bottom *Treasure Island*, 1896, illustrated edition courtesy of The Wandsworth Collection.
Top and opposite Illustrations © 2009 Michael Foreman, from *Treasure Island*, reproduced by permission of Pavilion Children's Books an imprint of Anova Books Ltd.

Florence and Bertha Upton

Florence Upton was an artist and the inventor of the Golliwogg (later Golliwog). With Bertha, Florence's mother, writing the text, and Florence creating the illustrations, mother and daughter worked together on 13 Golliwogg adventures.

The first book, *The Adventures of Two Dutch Dolls and a Golliwogg*, published for Christmas 1895, was followed by *The Golliwogg's Bicycle Club*, 1896. Other books included *The Golliwogg in War*, 1899, *The Golliwogg's Auto-Go-Cart*, 1901, and *The Golliwogg's Circus*, 1903, until the last, *Golliwogg in the African Jungle*, which was published in 1909.

Florence's style was simple, using black outline with blocks of colour and some shading. She used various techniques to create some shallow depth—the line of soldiers, and the explosion in *The Golliwogg in War!*, the depth created in *The Golliwogg's Auto-Go-Cart* by placing the figures in the foreground and background.

Now over a century old, the Golliwogg was a controversial figure from the outset; on first meeting, he frightens the Dutch dolls, though he quickly wins them over.

From the second book onwards, Golliwogg moved to being the central figure and the series became hugely popular. It was a favourite of Edgar Osborne as a child (founder of the Osborne Collection of Early Children's Books at the Toronto Public Library, Canada).

As popular as the Golliwogg was, he was based on a racist stereotype which brings the series into highly controversial ground with modern audiences. Many believe that the Golliwogg should be remembered fondly as a cultural artifact, whilst others see it as a grotesque relic from a time of blatant racism.

Florence and Bertha did not copyright their 'invention'; with the Golliwogg a hugely popular figure in children's literature and in the public domain, many toy manufacturers and companies of all types began to use him in their marketing and branding. In Britain, James Robertson & Sons adopted the Golly as a central part of its brand. Florence Upton's own Golliwogg, and her Dutch dolls, are now at the Museum of Childhood in East London. Despite the use of the Golliwogg in such a diverse range of contexts, the shape, colour and appearance of all Golliwoggs since Florence's remain broadly the same, with the familiar wide mouth, black skin colour, and bow tie, red jacket and stripey trousers.

Left and opposite *The Adventures of Two Dutch Dolls*, illustrated by Florence K Upton.
Above *The Golliwogg's Circus*, illustrated by Florence K Upton.
All images courtesy of The Wandsworth Collection.

The Wind in the Willows
Kenneth Grahame

Kenneth Grahame's Arcadian world of *The Wind in the Willows* plays on a tradition of Victorian etiquette yet is still enjoyed by new readers today. Jumping between slow and calm riverside retreats to sudden bursts of action and intrigue, *The Wind in the Willows* encapsulates the perfect summer holiday where we can relax for just long enough before getting sleepy, and then become swept off in an adventure.

The book was first published in 1908 as just Grahame's text. Although illustrated editions quickly appeared, a 1931 edition drawn by EH Shepard of *Winnie the Pooh* fame is perhaps the most widely known today. AA Milne, author of the Pooh books, also adapted the stories into a successful theatre production, *Toad of Toad Hall*. Shepard's detailed but innocent sketches capture the playful humour of Grahame's text, and although Grahame sadly never lived to see the finished work, he loved Shepard's characterisations and congratulated him for bringing the characters to life, telling him "I'm so glad you made them real!."

The Wind in the Willows' classic status has meant that it has been returned to and reinterpreted by famous illustrators again and again, thus ensuring its popularity with new generations of readers. Illustrators as varied as Val Biro, Inga Moore and Michael Foreman have all turned their talents to recreating the famous riverbank tales.

The Wind in the Willows Kenneth Grahame 81

Val Biro's 1983 edition is a playful retelling of the stories with witty visual accompaniments to the more comical events of the book.

Michael Foreman was driven to take his watercolour brush to the tales after being inspired by reading Grahame's letters to his young son Alistair. Two of these letters accompany the finished book and tell an early version of Toad's escapades as a washerwoman. Foreman's sumptuous envisioning of the adventures are brightly coloured, often leaning on greens and blues to represent riverside life, and full of an energy that brings the story the same vitality that it possessed when first published over a century ago.

Opposite top *The Wind in the Willows* © The Estate of EH Shepard with permission of Curtis Brown Group Ltd.
Opposite bottom and below *Tales from the Wind in the Willows*, illustrations by Val Biro © 1983. Reproduced by permission of the artist.
Above Illustrations © 2009 Michael Foreman, from *The Wind in the Willows*, reproduced by permission of Pavilion Children's Books an imprint of Anova Books Ltd.

Winnie the Pooh
EH Shepard

Winnie the Pooh and friends are today still amongst the most famous of children's books characters. Pooh, Piglet, Tiger and crew's popularity has continued to last decade by decade, and although many would now recognise them primarily through Disney's interpretations of the band of cuddly toys, EH Shepard's original illustrations are still well-known and loved.

Born in 1879, EH Shepard knew from an early age that he wanted to become an artist and his dream as a young man was to work for *Punch* magazine as a political cartoonist.

After many attempts at publication, *Punch* finally accepted two of Shepard's sketches. It was through *Punch* that Shepard came to produce his most famous work for AA Milne's *Winnie the Pooh*. Milne was also contributing verse and essays to the magazine and asked a friend to recommend an artist to illustrate his collection of children's poems, *When We Were Young*. Shepard's name was put forward, although Milne initially disliked Shepard's work for the book, describing him as "perfectly useless" as an artist.

The book and Shepard's illustrations were however a success, and Milne grew to appreciate his style. Shepard illustrated the subsequent Pooh titles: *Winnie the Pooh* and *The House at Pooh Corner*. Milne's motivation for writing the books came from his son Christopher Robin Milne, whose beloved toys populated the tales. The Milne family lived at Cotchford Farm in Sussex and the surrounding area of Ashdown Forest became the setting of the now famous "100 Aker Wood". Although Pooh was inspired by Christopher Robin's teddy, the bear in the books was actually drawn from Shepard's son's bear, Growler.

Shepard's simple but balanced line drawings managed to convey the innocence of the characters, with emphasis on their shape and form rather than detail or facial expression. Pooh's upturned nose indicates his inquisitiveness, which relates to a child's own trends of thought and behaviour.

Like Milne, who came to resent the fact that his greatest success was a children's book and whose plays and more serious works never achieved the same fame, Shepard begrudged the fact that "the bear of very little brain" overshadowed his other work. He saw his picture-book illustrations as a sideline, and wanted to be remembered for something more substantial. However Shepard viewed his own works for children books, he created one of the most universally loved and recognisable characters of the twentieth century, and Pooh is today as popular as ever.

Image copyright © The Estate of EH Shepard with permission of Curtis Brown Group Ltd.

The Wonderful Wizard of Oz
L Frank Baum

One of the most famous 'voyage and return' tales of all time, *The Wonderful Wizard of Oz*, like *Alice in Wonderland*, has remained in children's hearts since its first publication due to copious re-workings that have ensured its lasting popularity.

The story is heavily influenced by classic fairy tales and the works of the Brothers Grimm, but Baum wanted to create an 'American fairy tale' that stayed true to the genre but left out the darker, more sinister aspects of earlier fairy tales. Baum wanted to channel the success of Lewis Carroll's *Alice*, whom he saw as the main source of that books popularity. He believed that children needed someone with whom they could identify, and thus Dorothy was created.

Baum and the book's original illustrator WW Denslow were friends and collaborators before they came to work on *The Wonderful Wizard of Oz* together.

Opposite top Illustrations © 2009 Michael Foreman, from *The Wizard of Oz*, reproduced by permission of Pavilion Children's Books an imprint of Anova Books Ltd.
Opposite bottom *The Wonderful Wizard of Oz and Father Goose*, c.1900, colour lithography by Denslow, William Wallace, 1856–1919. Private Collection/Archives Charmet/The Bridgeman Art Library
Above *The Wizard of Oz* © 2008 by Graham Rawle, reproduced by permission of the artist.

Above *The Wizard of Oz* © 2008 by Graham Rawle, reproduced by permission of the artist.
Opposite *The Wonderful Wizard of Oz*, © 2001 Robert Sabuda,
Published by Simon and Schuster in 2001.

The design of the book was incredibly rich for the time, with illustrations on every page, colour plate illustrations and backgrounds and foregrounds in different colours. Baum's sense of humour suited Denslow's style, and the style likewise suited the text. The book was imagined by the two men as a single entity, rather than text and imagery existing separately and then being brought together.

Published at the turn of the twentieth century, *The Wizard of Oz* pre-empted much of the coming century's ever increasing reliance on technology, and its effect on consumer capitalism. It also explores the idea of an all-powerful leader and the propaganda that is necessary to support such a figure.

The Wizard of Oz was by far Baum's biggest success, and although he twice attempted to write a definitive end to the series, the fans would not allow it. In his later years Baum was forced to continue writing sequels, such as *Ozma of Oz* and *Tik-Tok of Oz*, in order to

support himself. The later books were illustrated by John R Neil who continued to produce work for reprints of the *Oz* books into the 1940s, as Baum and Denslow's relationship had since deteriorated.

Nowadays, the film and Broadway adaptations introduce new generations of readers to the book, which has been illustrated by many modern illustrators including an intricate pop-up version by Robert Sabuda. Michael Foreman's *Oz* plays on Denslow's original illustrations but with modern influences and full blown watercolour skylines and Emerald cityscapes, whilst Victor Ambrus brought an Eastern European flavour to the American classic. Graham Rawle recreated a miniature version of Oz sets made with old containers and Christmas decorations and populated with handcrafted dolls as the characters. Rawle photographed the results and blended them with cut outs to create a collage edition of *The Wizard of Oz* which is witty and camp at the same time as being incredibly loyal to the original story.

Contemporary Children's Books

Lisa Sainsbury

During the immediate post-war years a number of influential visual texts and characters appeared that have shaped the terrain of contemporary children's literature.

Comic-strips had been gaining in popularity and though not read exclusively by children, or necessarily intended for them, this visual form was central to the reading experience of many young readers from the 1940s onwards. Between the late 1930s and 1960s, the giants of the US comics industry, DC Comics and Marvel, produced some of the most potent icons of the Western World; Superman, Batman, Captain America, Wonder Woman, Spider Man and the Hulk battled to satisfy the appetites of a war-ravaged world for heroism on a superhuman and indestructible scale. In the UK, the anti-hero prevailed in comic-strips of a more comedic and down-to-earth flavour than that of the brash US strips. Although destined to become a star of British television from the late 1950s to 1970s, Captain Horatio Pugwash, the comic-strip creation of John Ryan, first appeared in *The Eagle* in 1950. The most noteworthy comic-strip creation of this era was "Dennis the Menace". Created by Dave Law in 1951, "Dennis the Menace" revolutionised *The Beano* and his escapades with Gnasher the Dog (who joined Dennis in 1968) continue to entertain children in the only weekly narrative comic still available on British news-stands in the twenty-first century. Dennis' image has altered significantly over time, illustrated by David Sutherland and David Parkins after Law, but his scraggy black hair and red-black sweater have remained a constant. Dennis is also recognisable as a scruffy, naughty schoolboy in the tradition of

Opposite Illustration from *The Beano Annual*, 1999 © DC Thompson & Co., Ltd.
Above *Captain Pugwash*, text and illustrations copyright © John Ryan, 1957, first published by Frances Lincoln 2007.

Crompton's William and he has a contemporary counterpart in Francesca Simon's *Horrid Henry* (illustrated by Tony Ross's anarchic mix of line and colour), who first appeared in 1994. *Bunty*, a weekly comic for girls, was established in 1958 and produced its final edition in 2001; one of its most well-liked strips was "The Four Marys", developed in the convention of school stories popularised by Angela Brazil, Elinor Brent-Dyer and Enid Blyton.

Some unforgettable moments of book illustration energised this period of children's literature and a number of illustrators such as Edward Ardizzone spanned the war years, continuing to produce work into the post-war period. Garth Williams' witty lines chart triumph and loss in EB White's *Charlotte's Web*, 1952, while Diana Stanley captured the minute detail of the Borrowers' world in Mary Norton's *The Borrowers*, 1952. Pauline Baynes' sharp line drawings gave life to CS Lewis' *Narnia Chronicles*, 1950–1956, to be followed later by Christian Birmingham's sensitive rendition of *The Lion the Witch and the Wardrobe*, 1998, in rich, glowing pastels. In the USA Don Freeman brought Astrid Lindgren's work to new audiences in his illustrations for *Bill Bergson Lives Dangerously*, 1954, while Susan Einzig's perceptive pen and ink illustrations for Philippa Pearce's *Tom's Midnight Garden*, 1958, launched her career in the UK. Mervyn Peake illustrated numerous children's classics, including *The Hunting of the Snark*, 1941, *Alice's Adventures in Wonderland* and *Through the Looking-Glass*, 1946, *Grimms' Household Tales*, 1946, and *The Swiss Family Robinson*, 1949; his dexterous line drawings for Stevenson's *Treasure Island*, 1949, encapsulate the narrator's ambivalent attitude to Long John Silver. Indeed, the illustration of children's classics has proved a coming-of-age for many

Just William, text © Richmal C Ashbee, illustration © 1922, by The Thomas Henry Fisher Estate.

illustrators and countless revisionings of important works of children's literature emerged during the twentieth century, each version interpreting the story differently. Tove Jansson, 1966, Ralph Steadman, 1967 and 1972, Anthony Browne, 1988,

> **❝ Some unforgettable moments of book illustration energised this period of children's literature and a number of illustrators such as Edward Ardizzone spanned the war years, continuing to produce work into the post-war period. ❞**

Tony Ross, 1994, Helen Oxenbury, 1999 and Lisbeth Zwerger, 1999, have each produced outstanding versions of Carroll's *Alice* books; Grahame's *The Wind in the Willows* has been rendered by John Burningham, 1983, Patrick Benson, 1994, and Michael Foreman, 2001; Victor Ambrus, 1992, and Chris Riddell, 2004, have tackled *Gulliver's Travels*; while WW Denslow's 1900 interpretation of Baum's *The Wonderful Wizard of Oz* has been followed by Michael Foreman, 1990, Lisbeth Zwerger, 1996, and

Victor Ambrus, 1999. It is true that the verbal text of many of these books could stand alone, but there is no doubt that illustrative interpretations set up a dialogue with the narrative, reshaping familiar tales and rendering them anew.

Children's books of this period also threw up several enduring characters. Dressed in primary colours, Enid Blyton's *Noddy* was designed to be noticed when he first appeared in 1949 and, set against the backdrop

Illustration © 2004 Chris Riddell, from *Jonathan Swift's Gulliver*, retold by Martin Jenkins and illustrated by Chris Riddell.
Reproduced by permission of Walker Books Ltd, London SE11 5HJ.

of post-war privation, his instant commercial success is unsurprising. Blyton has continued to dominate bookshelves into the twenty-first century, but arguably it is Harmsen Van der Beek's vibrant, full-page illustrations of the Noddy books that acquired Blyton's nodding doll iconic status, rather than her laborious verbal text. Alf Proysen's *Mrs Pepperpot* emerged in Norway in 1957 (translations from 1959), and has been illustrated variously by Bjorn Berg, Nils Stodberg, Jens Ahlbom and David Arthur; Proysen's diminutive heroine also starred in her own animated series (as have many of the characters mentioned here) in Japan during the 1980s. Michael Bond's *Paddington* arrived at Paddington station in 1958, initially illustrated by Peggy Fortnum's loose and energetic line drawings; as Bond explains, "they captured Paddington's character completely—those sketchy drawings were of a living, breathing creature, with the spirit of Paddington about them: his incurable optimism, his gullibility".[1] Paddington was depicted in the 1970s by Fred Banbery in a series of *Paddington* picture-books, adapted from Bond's stories for very young readers, and during the 80s similarly adapted Paddington books were illustrated by David McKee, the creator of the children's TV animation, *Mr Benn* and *Elmer*, 1989. American illustrator, Bob Alley, is the most recent artist to take on Paddington and his pen and ink work fills the pages of Bond's latest book, *Paddington Here and Now*, 2008, written to celebrate Paddington's fiftieth anniversary.

In the field of picture-books a subdued palette characterises the texts of the 1940s and 50s, literally in terms of illustration and metaphorically in terms of content. Picture-books such as *Make Way for Ducklings*, 1941, and *Blueberries for Sal*, 1948, by American writer-illustrator Robert McCloskey offered an antidote to a world traumatised by two World Wars. In *Blueberries for Sal*, the blue and white lithographs lend a calming uniformity to this tale as Sal is separated from her mother and the amusing, sensitive illustrations are likely to defuse any anxiety the reader might experience. Sal herself is closely observed and McCloskey's ability to capture the child's movement through expressive line is not dissimilar to that of British artist, Shirley Hughes. Hughes gave life in pen and ink to Dorothy Edwards' *My Naughty Little Sister* stories in the 1950s and Hughes' own picture-books are populated by the mucky, cheeky, mischievous children, such as those in *Lucy and Tom's*

> **❝ Blyton has continued to dominate bookshelves into the twenty-first century, but arguably it is Harmsen Van der Beek's vibrant, full-page illustrations of the *Noddy* books that acquired Blyton's nodding doll iconic status. ❞**

Day, 1960, *Dogger*, 1977, and *Alfie Gets in First*, 1981, who can be recognised in many British families, schools or local neighbourhoods. Hughes' vibrant sketches and verbal text capture the comic potential in domestic life, and this everyday humour also infuses the work of Canadian illustrator, Margaret Bloy Graham in her illustrations for Gene Zion's *Harry the Dirty Dog*, 1956. The muted ochre and olive background that follows Harry through his adventures has become almost as memorable as Harry himself, mirroring trends in fashion and textiles of the period. Splashes of red offset the ochre and monochrome lines in the artwork of Swiss artist Roger Duvoisin for Louise Fatio's *The Happy Lion*, 1950. Discrimination directed at the happy lion is quickly overcome through the triumph of unprejudiced childhood in this simple story, but Duvoisin's use of colour is a reminder of the harmful potential in prejudice; it is clear then that even during this seemingly benign period in children's literature, artists and writers recognise the potential for picture-books to deal with complex ideas.

Illustrations © 1998 Christian Birmingham, from *The Lion the Witch and the Wardrobe*, written by CS Lewis.

Challenging the reserved tone of post-war picture-books through the use of bright colour and shapes defined by bold, black line, Dick Bruna's *Miffy* books (from 1955) are designed for small hands in the reader friendly tradition of Beatrix Potter's *Peter Rabbit* books. The influence of Bruna's clean, bright design can also be seen in the Helen Nicoll's *Meg and Mog* books (from 1972), illustrated by Jan Pieńkowski, Roger Hargreaves' *Mr Men* (from 1971) and *Little Miss* books (from 1981), Eric Hill's *Spot*, 1980, and Lucy Cousins' *Maisy* books, from1990. Perhaps the master of bold, both in terms of zany images and elaborate rhyming narratives, Theodor Seuss Geisel, better known as Dr Seuss, published his internationally renowned *The Cat in the Hat* in 1957. *The Cat in the Hat* was Geisel's response to the challenge of writing and illustrating a primer for use in schools, which would stimulate and excite young readers; that he was limited to 220 words designed to aid literacy renders the success of his *I Can Read* books all the more remarkable (though it may also explain the sometimes cumbersome and long-winded nature of his verbal texts). Like

Above Illustrations © Mercis 1953–2009, from *Miffy at the Gallery* by Dick Bruna.

Johann Amos Comenius in the seventeenth century, Geisel recognised the important role of illustration in language acquisition and education generally; he went on to edit several books in the *I Can Read* series, working with authors and illustrators such as Stan and Jan Berenstain on *The Big Honey Hunt*, 1962, and other titles in their prolific *Berenstain Bear* series. The success of this influential reading series is further explained by the presence of several classic texts on its list produced by critically acclaimed and award-winning authors/illustrators. *Bed-Time for Frances*, 1960, is the first of Russell Hobans' Frances books featuring the toddlerish foibles of the eponymous badger heroine; the first in the series was illustrated by Garth Williams, though Lillian Hoban illustrated subsequent books. In *Bread and Jam for Frances*, 1964, Lillian Hoban's reassuring pastel backgrounds and soft pencil sketches complement Russell Hoban's astutely observed narrative about the domestic challenges experienced by many young children. Lillian illustrated many of Russell Hoban's books and her cross-hatched lines for *The Mouse and His Child*, 1967, capture the toys' pursuit of self-winding with controlled sensitivity. Lillian also created her own books for the *I Can Read* series, the best known of which are probably those about *Arthur the Chimpanzee*, such as *Arthur's Honey Bear*, 1974. Arnold Lobel's *Frog and Toad* books (from

Is Maisy
in the
boat?

Opposite bottom and this page Illustration © 1999 Lucy Cousins, from *Where is Maisy?* by Lucy Cousins, Maisy™. Maisy is a registered trademark of Walker Books Ltd, London. Reproduced by permission of Walker Books Ltd, London SE11 5HJ.

"Ladybird books echoed the dominant ideologies of the period, reflecting the experiences of middle class, white children and conforming to the patriarchal model of domestic goddesses and workplace fathers."

1970) employ a series of dun-toned sketches to offset these gentle, pastoral tales of friendship in the tradition of Beatrix Potter, Kenneth Grahame and Mark Twain. Maurice Sendak's partnership with Else Holmelund Minarik for their *Little Bear* books (from 1957) is also noteworthy, for Sendak was at this point developing his career as an illustrator before turning to his own picture-books in the 1960s.

In the UK, one publishing company was set to dominate the early reading experiences of generations of British children; Wills and Hepworth (eventually becoming Ladybird Books in 1971) published their first 'Ladybird' book, *Bunnikin's Picnic Party* in 1940. After the Second World War, Wills and Hepworth expanded the range of their Ladybird series to include fairy tales, nature books, biblical stories and many others. Several established illustrators worked on these series, confirming the significance accorded to plentiful and accomplished visual images in early learning and reading: Allen Seaby (author/illustrator of pony stories from the 1920s to 40s) illustrated the *British Birds and their Nests* titles in the 1950s; Frank Hampson (creator of Dan Dare for *The Eagle* in the 50s) illustrated Ladybird's popular *Nursery Rhyme* series during the 60s; and CF Tunnicliffe (illustrator of Williamson's *Tarka the Otter*, 1927, and Brook Bonds tea cards, collected by young people in the 1950s and 60s) illustrated the *What to Look For* books in the 60s. Ladybird's most successful series was their Key Words Reading Scheme, popularly known as the *Peter and Jane* books, which energised the UK education market when it was launched in 1964 just as the *I Can Read* series did in the USA. It should be noted, however, that while moving forward the pedagogic market, the Ladybird books echoed the dominant ideologies of

the period, reflecting the experiences of middle class, white children and conforming to the patriarchal model of domestic goddesses and workplace fathers.

Essentially, the post-war years represent a period of consolidation in the world of children's literature, investing firmly in the importance of early years education and offering young readers a rich visual dimension to their novels, primers, comics and picture-books. With some exceptions, such as Crockett Johnson's ground-breaking *Harold and the Purple Crayon*, 1955, in which the infant Harold crafts his own world using a purple crayon and his imagination, there is a conservatism at work during the 40s and 50s. Children's literature of this period largely endorses the Western values that prevailed prior to the First and Second World Wars and frequently offers a haven of calm and reassurance to a world weary of destruction, loss and deprivation. That children's illustration was beginning to be more widely recognised in the UK is confirmed by the establishment in 1955 of the Kate Greenaway Medal for illustration; a recognition accorded earlier in the USA with the foundation of the Caldecott Medal in 1937. So, after this era of relative calm, the picture-book was due to explode in a riot of innovation as the 1960s dawned and a new generation of artists, writers and picture-book creators came to the attention of critics, parents, educators and enthusiastic young audiences alike.

Illustration © 1966 Val Biro, *Gumdrop: The Adventures of a Vintage Car* by Val Biro. Reproduced by permission of the artist.

The 1960s' Riot of Creativity

Commentators seem to agree that the 1960s is the point at which the picture-book really settled into a recognisable and important literary form. As David Lewis says of the picture-book's evolution in *Reading Contemporary Picturebooks*:

Its emergence from other forms of printed matter such as chapbooks, toy books and comics has been gradual and rather uneven... and it is not until the second half of the twentieth century that the picturebook was fully formed. Since the 1960s more and more picturebooks have been published every year so that now, in the early twenty-first century, it is beginning to feel as if they have always been there.[2]

A number of influential picture-books were published in the 1960s and this period represents the second golden age of children's picture-books and illustration. Some of the most important artists of contemporary children's literature were awarded the Greenaway Medal during the 1960s, marking the beginning of prolific and influential careers—recipients included: John Burningham for *Borka*, 1963; Raymond Briggs for his irreverent *Mother Goose Treasury*, 1967; Helen Oxenbury for her illustrations of Lear's *The Quangle Wangle's Hat*, 1969, and Margaret Mahy's *The Dragon of an Ordinary Family*, 1969; and Charles Keeping for *Charley, Charlotte and the Golden Canary*, 1967. In the USA Leo Lionni and Evaline Ness received several Caldecott Honours each for their work, while Uri Shulevitz scooped the Caldecott Medal with *The Fool of the World and the Flying Ship*, 1968—a Russian folktale retold by Arthur Ransome—as did William Steig for *Sylvester and the Magic Pebble*, 1969, his tale of transformation, loss and recovery (Steig also went on to create *Shrek!* in 1990). Further books of note that have acquired classic status since the 1960s include Shel Silverstein's *The Giving Tree*, 1965, Richard Scarry's *Busy, Busy World*, 1965, Val Biro's *Gumdrop*, 1966, Don Freeman's *Corduroy*, 1968, and Judith Kerr's *The Tiger That Came to Tea*, 1968, soon to be joined by Mog in 1970, the well-loved feline who Kerr allowed a graceful death in *Goodbye Mog*, 2002. Though not picture-book heroes, *The Wombles* were familiar to most British households in late 60s and 70s. They were the creation of Elizabeth Beresford in *The Wombles*, 1968, illustrated by Margaret Gordon and produced for television by FilmFair in stop-motion animation from 1973.

Brian Wildsmith's ABC, 1962, was awarded the Greenaway Medal and is recognised as a text that set new standards in children's literature. New developments in printing technology allowed for colour to be reproduced more accurately than previously and hence the *ABC* is rich with painterly swirls of colour. Furthermore, the robust texture of Wildsmith's artwork refuses the sentimentality sometimes associated with the literature of early childhood. That Wildsmith's *ABC* is considered a landmark text is confirmed by Douglas Martin, who suggests that the "modern period" of picture-books, "can be dated conveniently from the appearance of *Brian Wildsmith's ABC* in 1962".[3] Wildsmith's 'U'nicorn is an especially powerful example of how the images that accompany each letter of the alphabet work as narrative catalyst; Wildsmith distances the horn most commonly associated with the Unicorn, focusing instead on the creature's backside. His Unicorn is presented from a fresh perspective, thus embracing narrative possibilities from fairy tale fantasies to buttock-clenching jokes. Wildsmith reveals that "I use what I call the Mozartian method. Mozart had an idea totally impregnated on his mind. And I work like that. For *ABC* I didn't make sketches or anything. I drew straight onto the page and painted on top of that in gouache. The turtle was drawn entirely in paint, without any pencil".[4] Wildsmith has gone on to create numerous, immediately recognizable picture-books, including *The Hare and The Tortoise*, 1966, *Professor Noah's Spaceship*, 1980, and *The Creation*, 1995.

Of course, Wildsmith is not alone in locating the humble ABC as a site of innovation and creativity; it

is recognised as a genre in its own right with a long history reaching back to the earliest days of children's literature. Maurice Sendak included an alphabet book, *Alligator's All Round*, in his *Nutshell Library*, 1962, which includes four miniature volumes for little people. Soaked in the parodic traditions of Hoffmann and Belloc, Edward Gorey's *The Gashleycrumb Tinies*,

1963, is a masterful black comedy, rehearsing the alphabetic death of its youthful protagonists with a delicious sense of rhyme and theatrical timing: "A is for Amy who fell down the stairs, B is for Basil assaulted by Bears"; Gorey's ABC is perhaps not intended for children, but surely enjoyed by all those who delight in the macabre.

Illustration © 1966 Val Biro, *Gumdrop: The Adventures of a Vintage Car* by Val Biro. Reproduced by permission of the artist.

unicorn
UNICORN

Dr Seuss's ABC appeared in 1963, soon followed by Helen Oxenbury's *ABC of Things*, 1967; while Shirley Hughes' alphabet books, *Lucy and Tom's ABC*, 1984, and *Alfie's ABC*, 1998, feature some of her most beloved characters. Mitsumasa Anno's unique take on the ABC format, *Anno's Alphabet*, 1974, encourages young readers to hunt down images hidden within the *trompe l'oeil*, 'wooden' letters on each page. This approach is typical of Anno's picture-books; *Anno's Upside Downers*, 1988, is another example, frequently inviting the reader to take an interactive role and to connect physically and playfully. In *The Z was Zapped*, 1987, Chris Van Allsburg presents each letter as a performer on the stage, appearing grandly from behind the swish of the curtain in his trademark black and white; a homage to Gorey is also possible given that in Act 2, "the B was badly bitten" and the accompanying image shows a bestial mouth slavering over the inert capital B. Christopher Wormell's *An Alphabet of Animals*, 1990, makes use of traditional printing methods, rendering the alphabet in block print. Manifestly, the ABC allows illustrators to demonstrate that narrative can be suggested by associative, visual play in which words are frequently withdrawn.

The publication of *Where the Wild Things Are* in 1963 (awarded the Caldecott Medal), confirmed Maurice Sendak as a leading figure in the world of picture-books and the books which followed, such as *In the*

Artwork from *Brian Wildsmith's ABC*, illustration © Brian Wildsmith, 1962, used by permission of Oxford University Press.

Night Kitchen, 1970, *Outside Over There*, 1981, and *We Are All in the Dumps with Jack and Guy*, 1993, sealed his reputation as one of the most important illustrators of his era. *Wild Things* is innovative in terms of content, expressing the psychological impact of a child's destructive anger (an emotion new to children's picture-books), and in terms of form, using the decreasing/increasing frames of each illustration to reflect Max's emotional journey. As Sendak explains of his work, "what interests me is what children do at a particular moment in their lives when there are no rules, no laws, when emotionally they don't know what is expected of them. In *Where the Wild Things Are*, Max gets mad. What do you do with getting mad?"; Sendak is

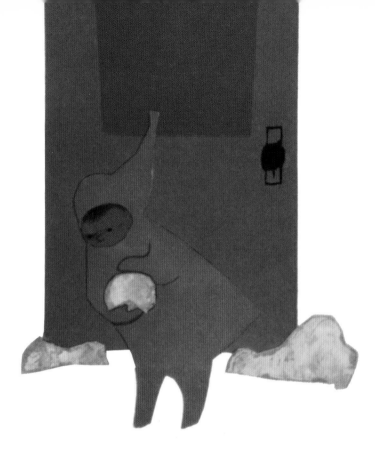

clearly conscious of the psychological dimensions of the experiences he attempts to convey.[5] Sendak's body of work also demonstrates his awareness of the cultural tradition within which he functions; references to Mozart can be found in *Outside Over There*, for example, and the influence of Caldecott and Cruikshank (among many other artists) is evident in many of his books. Sendak is open about these influences, revealing that the artist does not work alone, but in constant dialogue with other practitioners; he divulges that "my great and abiding love was William Blake, my teacher in all things"[6] and attributes the birth of the modern picture-book to Randolph Caldecott, looking back to those first golden days of children's literature as he pursues his own path as an extraordinary artist.[7]

Ezra Jack Keats won the Caldecott Medal for *The Snowy Day*, 1962, a simple tale of inner city life that conveys Peter's joy at freshly fallen snow. Significantly, this was the first time that an American illustrator had placed a black child in the focal role of a picture-book. Keats' experimental style is also notable, using a range of techniques (mixing collage and gouache, for example) to give his work a texture that conveys depth and atmosphere. Keats produced numerous picture-books, such as *Peter's Chair*, 1967,

Apt. 3, 1971 and *Dreams*, 1974, which give voice and recognition to children from a range of different cultures. The groundbreaking multi-culturalism of Keats' work contributed to a change of attitudes in the publishing world, giving an opening to artists from various cultures. John Steptoe, the African American author-illustrator, published *Stevie* in 1969, the tale of an only child's resentment when faced with the arrival of a foster brother. The verbal text of *Stevie* captures the cadence of African American English and Steptoe's luminous illustrations are surrounded by strong, black lines. Steptoe proceeded to publish a range of books concerned with life in the African American community and African folklore, including *Uptown*, 1970, *Daddy Is a Monster… Sometimes*, 1980, *The Story of Jumping Mouse*, 1984, and *Mufaro's Beautiful Daughters: An African Tale*, 1987.

Influenced by his mentors Leo Lionni (who published a number of philosophical books rendered in collage, such as *Swimmy* in 1963) and Ezra Jack Keats in the art of collage, Eric Carle is perhaps the best known collage artist of this era. *The Very Hungry Caterpillar*, 1969, has sold over 22 million copies and this tactile, playful book demonstrates an awareness of the way in which young children respond to books. Carle's books frequently include peritextual features (peripheral elements of the text, such as covers, borders, epigraphs, etc.) such as the die-cut pages in *The Very Hungry Caterpillar*, 1969, the importance of which is revealed by Margaret Higonnet:

> From "baby" books and "bath" books to "toy" books, an inventive commercial industry supports the introduction of children to books as objects to be handled, opened, explored, and eventually interpreted. The active appeal to all the senses of the small child… instructs us in an interactive relationship to books from an early age. Concrete devices such as cut-outs or scratch-and-sniff patches replicate features of narrative, or even function as substitute 'events' in the story sequence, events that can only 'happen' when the reader's finger does the work.[8]

As Higonnet and Carle evidently recognise, children are often quick to identify the peritext as a source of creative interactivity. Carle's subsequent

❝ Keats' experimental style is also notable, using a range of techniques (mixing collage and gouache, for example) to give his work a texture that conveys depth and atmosphere. ❞

Opposite and above *The Snowy Day*, © Ezra Jack Keats, 1962. Reproduced with special permission from the Ezra Jack Keats Foundation.

publications have included a range of techniques to stimulate young readers from pop-ups and moveables in *The Honeybee and the Robber*, 1981, to raised printing in *The Very Busy Spider*, 1984 and a chip that mimics the song of a cricket in *The Very Quiet Cricket*, 1990. Another influential text of the 1960s that recognised the importance of empowering and involving children was *Rosie's Walk*, 1968, by Pat Hutchins. Rather than relying on peritextual features, Hutchins makes use of counterpoint in the ironic gap between the visual and verbal narratives, allowing readers to recognise for themselves the comic antics of the fox that are consistently ignored by the dead-pan, verbal narration.

Although the 1960s is really the decade of the picture-book, a number of illustrative works appeared that have had a lasting impact on children's literature. The American illustrator, Nancy Ekholm Burkert produced a haunting, monochromatic vision of *James and the Giant Peach*, 1961, that sets a tragic tone for Dahl's text in complete contrast to Quentin Blake's more light-hearted approach of 1995. An important illustrator of the early twentieth century moving towards the end of his career, Ardizzone's inimitable style captured

Barney's longing and excitement in Clive King's *Stig of the Dump*, 1963. Emerging as important contemporary illustrators, Antony Maitland produced empathetic line drawings for Pearce's *A Dog So Small*, 1962, and energised Leon Garfield's *Jack Holborn*, 1964, while Charles Keeping produced dark, disturbing images for Alan Garner's *Elidor*, 1965. Keeping went on to produce haunting picture-books, interpreting classic works of literature through symbolic eddies of line, such as Alfred Noyes' *Highwayman*, 1981, *Beowulf*, 1982, and Tennyson's *The Lady of Shalott*, 1986. Tomi Ungerer illustrated Jeff Brown's *Flat Stanley*, 1964, of which Sendak enthuses: "[i]maginative manipulation of space and deft use of colour give the happy effect of pictures dancing through the book".[9] Jan

Pieńkowski made use of his commanding silhouette technique for Joan Aiken's *A Necklace of Raindrops*, 1968, winning the Greenaway Medal for their second collaboration on *The Kingdom Under the Sea*, 1971. Quentin Blake, the first children's laureate (appointed in 1999) also launched his career in the 1960s, illustrating Jules Verne's *Around the World in Eighty Days*, 1966, amongst many others and, along with Maurice Sendak, can be considered one of the most important illustrators of his generation. It is clear to see then that the 1960s truly provided the momentum for the profusion of picture-books that have appeared from the 1970s to the present day.

Below Illustration from *A Necklace of Raindrops* © Jan Pieńkowski 1968.
Opposite Illustration from *The Kingdom Under the Sea* © Jan Pieńkowski 1971.

Innovation in Contemporary Children's Books

I t is impossible in a short overview of contemporary visual texts to mention all of the important picture-books and illustrated texts that have appeared since the 1960s, so what follows explores some of the ways in which picture-book practitioners and illustrators have pushed at the boundaries of children's literature both in terms of form and content. Popular characters continue to emerge, though the lasting power of modern icons, such as Anthony Browne's *Willie the Wimp* (from 1985), Tony Ross' *Little Princess* (from 1986), Mick Inkpen's *Kipper* (from 1989), Axel Scheffler's *Gruffalo* (from 1999) and Ian Falconer's *Olivia* (from 2000), is yet to be established. Developments since the 60s confirm that picture-books are one of the most versatile and exciting literary forms. John Burningham's *Come Away from the Water, Shirley*, 1977, exploits the form of the picture-book to contrast adult and child experience, placing adult and child on opposing sides of each double-page

spread. David Macauley, an innovative practitioner who has influenced Chris Van Allsburg and David Wiesner, blurs fiction and non-fiction in *Unbuilding*, 1980, which charts the dismantling of the Empire State Building and Macauley challenges picture-book convention through his testing approach to narrative in *Black and White*, 1990. Jan Ormerod demonstrates her understanding of the form when discussing her multi-layered version of *The Story of Chicken Licken*, 1988, which depicts school-children performing the tale: "[m]aking a picture-book is often a matter of finding solutions to the design problems presented by the story".[10] Faith Ringgold's *Tar Beach*, 1991, is an urban dreamscape that transforms quilt to picture-book in a piece of remediation that blends seamlessly the artwork of the quilt with that of the picture-book. Lane Smith and Jon Scieszka blur the role of author and illustrator in *The Stinky Cheese Man and Other Fairly Stupid Tales*, 1992, as every aspect of their postmodern picture-book, from contents to back-page blurb, is drawn into the narrative chaos. Perspective becomes an essential part of narrative development in David McKee's *Charlotte's Piggy Bank*, 1996, and *Madlenka*, 2000, by Peter Sis, both practitioners recognising that the ways in which the viewer sees the story can contribute to meaning. In Sara Fanelli's inventive hands the picture-book looks like a diary in terms of design and content; *Dear Diary*, 2000, is filled with child-like doodles and functions as a diary for its central characters. *The Three Pigs*, 2001, winning David Wiesner his second Caldecott Medal, is an intertextual tour de force that collapses the boundaries of picture-book structure as the three pigs escape the wolf by fleeing the very pages of their own story. Illustrators have also fused more traditional methods with computer technology; Lauren Child works fluidly with computer generated graphics in *Clarice Bean That's Me*, 1999, for example. Essentially, these practitioners have helped the picture-book form to evolve into an exciting and challenging medium.

In the UK, Janet and Allan Ahlberg have been at the forefront of developments in the picture-book, fully exploiting the potential of the form to stimulate and delight young readers. *Each Peach Pear Plum*, 1978, was awarded the Greenaway Medal and its game of intertextual 'I Spy' rewards the young reader's

Tony Ross

I Want My Potty

wider knowledge of traditional tales with familiar characters such as Cinderella and Robin Hood secreted on every page. Many practitioners have recognised the close relationship between game and picture-book, encouraging readers to hunt for narrative clues in detailed visual images.

Opposite Text © 1999 Julia Donaldson, illustrations © 1999 Axel Scheffler, from *The Gruffalo*.
Above Text and illustrations © 1986 Tony Ross, from *I Want My Potty* by Tony Ross. Reproduced by permission of Andersen Press Ltd.
Overleaf *Kipper* by Mick Inkpen, text and illustrations © 1991 Mick Inkpen. Reproduced by permission of Hodder and Stoughton Limited.

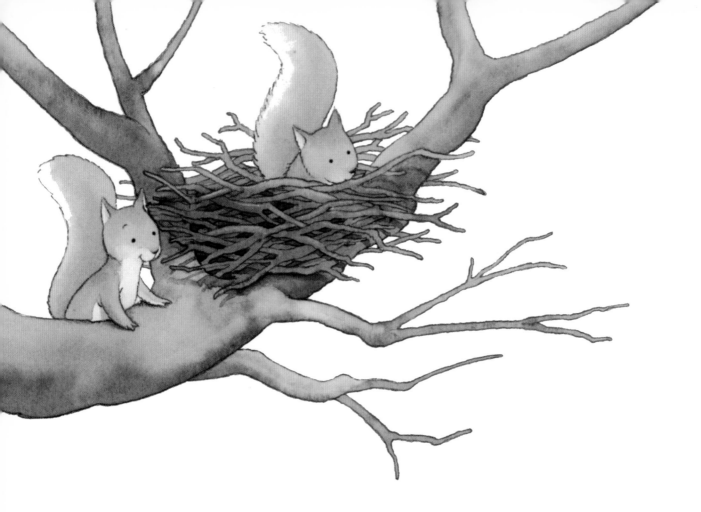

The squirrels had made their nest
out of sticks.

'I will build myself a stick nest!'
said Kipper. But Kipper's nest was
not very good. He could only find...

...three sticks!

Further examples include *Anno's Journey*, 1978, and *Anno's Animals*, 1979, by Mitsumasa Anno, Anthony Browne's *Piggy Book*, 1986, Martin Handford's *Where's Wally?*, 1987, Quentin Blake's *Cockatoos*, 1994, and *The Baby Who Wouldn't Go To Bed*, 1996, by Helen Cooper. In the Ahlberg's own *Peepo!*, 1981, another childhood game is foregrounded as domestic life of the 1940s is gradually revealed through peep holes in the centre of each page. Among the most highly acclaimed and commercially successful of contemporary moveable texts is the Ahlbergs' *The Jolly Postman*, 1986— followed by *The Jolly Christmas Postman*, 1991, and *The Jolly Pocket Postman*, 1995—a text that utilises a composite structure of literary text and toy to gain access to its fictional landscape.

In *Caldecott & Co.*, Maurice Sendak implies that the contemporary pop-up book is a 'poor relation' to the masterful mechanical books of such artists as Lothar Meggendorfer, who produced his mechanicals in the late nineteenth century.[11] Nonetheless, the pop-up book (the generic term now conferred on most movable picture-books) could be said to be undergoing a renaissance, judging by the proliferation of mechanical wizardry between the covers of numerous children's books. Robert Crowther's international bestseller, *The Most Amazing Hide-and-Seek Alphabet Book*, 1977, invited children to lift and pull its bold, black letters in order to reveal the 'L'obster, 'Q'uail and 'N'ewt. Jan Pieńkowski gained another Greenaway Medal for his hilarious and ingenious pop-up book, *Haunted House*, 1979, which moves skeletons in the cupboard from the metaphoric to literal. In the USA, the prolific paper engineer Robert Sabuda has created a number of intricate versions of classic texts, including *The Moveable Mother Goose*, 1999, *The Wonderful Wizard of Oz*, 2000, *Alice's Adventures in Wonderland*, 2003, *The Chronicles of Narnia*, 2007, and *Peter Pan*, 2008. Contemporary authors have also worked with Sabuda, rendering their artwork in pop-up form, including Tomie dePaola in *Brava, Strega Nona!*, 2008, with Matthew Reinhart, Sabuda's frequent collaborator. Reinhart has also worked with Maurice Sendak and Arthur Yorinks to produce *Mommy?*, 2006, the first pop-up version of Sendak's work, suggesting that Sendak has found a contemporary paper engineer to succeed the legendary Meggendorfer.

Layouts for *The Most Amazing Hide and Seek Alphabet*, by Robert Crowther © 1977 Robert Crowther, courtesy of the Seven Stories Collection.

Above and opposite left *Haunted House* © Jan Pieńkowski 1979.
Reproduced by permission of Walker Books Ltd, London SE11 5HJ.

many times, employing it in *Ethel and Ernest*, 1998, the first British biography to be created in comic strip. Other contemporary artists to use the comic-strip format include: Uderzo and Goscinny, whose *Asterix the Gaul*, 1959, spawned the internationally renowned series of graphic novels; Art Spiegelman in his anthropomorphised account of the holocaust and its aftermath, *Maus I*, 1986, and *Maus II*, 1991; Posy Simmonds in *Fred*, 1987; Satoshi Kitamura in *Comic Adventures of Boots*, 2002; and Marcia Williams, who has re-told numerous classic tales through comic-strip, including *The Adventures of Robin Hood*, 1995, and *Charles Dickens and Friends*, 2002.

Raymond Briggs' best known work, *The Snowman*, 1978, is a tale of friendship and loss expressed in wordless panels of subdued pastels. The wordless picture-book is a specialist form, widely misunderstood by adults who associate the form with infancy and pre-reading. Wordless texts are actually extremely challenging for young readers, who must piece together the narrative from the visual clues provided and the wordless format also makes great

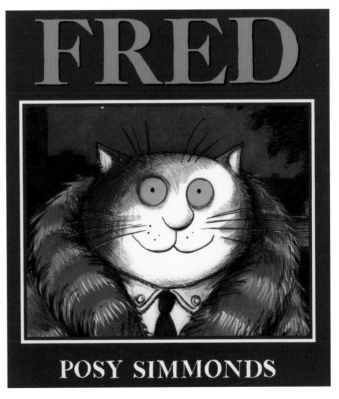

A British illustrator who has explored the full potential of the picture-book during his illustrative career is Raymond Briggs. His early work as an illustrator during the 1960s is mostly rendered in simple line drawing; a technique that Briggs returns to for political force in later picture-books such as *The Tin-pot Foreign General and the Old Iron Woman*, 1984. Briggs learnt more about the dynamics of the picture-book through collaboration with Elfrida Vipont in *The Elephant and the Bad Baby*, 1969, going on to create his own picture-book, *Jim and the Beanstalk* in 1970. Briggs pioneered the comic book form in the UK, earning his second Greenaway medal, for *Father Christmas*, 1973; as Philip Pullman reveals, Briggs stumbled into using the comic-strip as a way of including more narrative when he found that he had too much material to be accommodated in the standard picture-book format.[12] Briggs subsequently returned to this form

Right Reproduced from *Fred* © Posy Simmonds by permission of United Agents Ltd. on behalf of the author.

Above Reproduced from *Fred* © Posy Simmonds by permission
of United Agents Ltd. on behalf of the author.
Opposite Illustration © 2002 Marcia Williams, from *Charles Dickens
and Friends* by Marcia Williams. Reproduced by permission of Walker
Books Ltd, London SE11 5HJ.

demands upon artists who cannot rely on verbal text to move the story on. Those artists who have successfully conveyed stories in pictures alone have created some of the most evocative and expressive works of children's literature—these include: *Up & Up*, 1979, by Shirley Hughes; Jan Ormerod's *Sunshine*, 1981, and *Moonlight*, 1982; *Clown*, 1995, by Quentin Blake; Barbara Lehman's *The Red Book*, 2004, and *The Arrival*, 2006, by Shaun Tan. Several of these silent texts employ the panel format of comic-strip, thus allowing illustrators more time and space to tell their tales. The US illustrator, David Wiesner is one of the most original contemporary practitioners on the wordless scene. Wiesner's books build up a storyboard of images and offer a range of perspectives that lend his books

cinematic vision; for example, *Free Fall*, 1988, weaves a fluid dreamscape of images inspired by MC Esher and Lewis Carroll. Wiesner was awarded the Caldecott Medal for (the almost wordless) *Tuesday*, 1991, the comic, nocturnal adventure of a colony of frogs that zoom through the night on flying lily pads. One of the most unusual takes on the wordless picture-book is Chris Van Allsburg's, *The Mysteries of Harris Burdick*, 1984, a collection of illustrations with no story to accompany them; the potential for story lies with the reader alone.

The final panel of *The Snowman* is one of the most moving in children's literature, as the young boy is forced to confront his melted companion. Like many

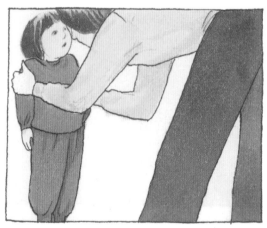
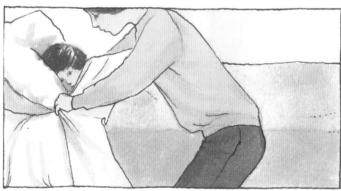

> **Those artists who have successfully conveyed stories in pictures alone have created some of the most evocative and expressive works of children's literature.**

contemporary illustrators, Briggs refuses to shield children from reality, remarking that he is not interested in "sweet innocent pink and blue baby stuff".[13] Picturebooks are frequently associated with early childhood and, as such, with notions of innocence and protection. However, many illustrators and authors have challenged this perspective and presented young readers with a more rounded view of human experience. Practitioners have also started to imply an older readership for their books, challenging the perception that picturebooks are only for those who cannot properly read, or lack sophisticated reading skills. As in *The Snowman*, death has been confronted by a range of artists: John Burningham's *Granpa*, 1984, movingly evokes Granpa's death through the washed out image of his empty chair, while black humour is the prevailing tone in Chris Raschka's *Arlene Sardine*, 1998, and *Egg Drop*, 2002, by Mini Grey. Although anger is commonly associated with early childhood, it is still relatively rare to find these emotions explored in literature for the young, but there are some powerful examples of books that confront childish rage, such as: Judith Viorst's *Alexander and the Terrible, Horrible, No Good, Very Bad Day*, 1972, illustrated by Ray Cruz; Satoshi Kitamura's *Angry Arthur*, 1982, and *When Sophie Gets Angry, Really Really Angry*, 1999, by Molly Bang. While melancholy is typically absent from books for the youngest of readers, this emotion has been sensitively portrayed in Shaun Tan's book about depression, *The Red Tree*, 2001, and by Quentin Blake in *Michael Rosen's Sad Book*, 2004, in which Rosen explores the grief he experienced on the death of his son.

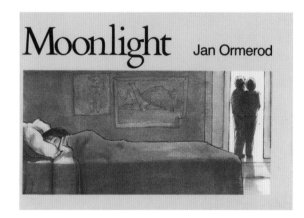

Opposite, top and middle *Sunshine*, illustrations © Jan Ormerod 1981, first published by Frances Lincoln, 2005. *Moonlight*, illustrations © Jan Ormerod 1982, first published by Frances Lincoln, 2004.
Bottom Text and illustrations © 1984 John Burningham, from *Granpa* by John Burningham. Reprinted by permission of the Random House Group Ltd.

One of the most damaging experiences known to humankind, war and human conflict, has been approached differently by a range of artists. Michael Foreman resorts to humour to convey his political message in *War and Peas*, 1974, and his autobiographical account of the Second World War in *War Boy*, 1989, is edged with nostalgia; in *Rose Blanche*, Roberto Innocenti's evocation of a young German girl's discovery of a Nazi concentration camp close to her home is unflinching, drawing on a famous image from the Warsaw ghetto for one of its central scenes.[14] Raymond Briggs has also confronted the politics of war in several books, most famously dealing with fallout from nuclear holocaust in *When the Wind Blows*, 1982. Issues relevant to contemporary society have also been explored in picture-books; Robert Munsch challenged fairy tale assumptions in *The Paper Bag Princess*, 1980, illustrated by Michael Martchenko, while *Princess Smartypants*, 1986, is just one of Babette Cole's irreverent forays into gender politics; homelessness is confronted in Libby Hathorn's *Way Home*, 1994, illustrated in dark tones by Gregory Rogers; and issues related to emigration are dealt with in Allen Say's *Grandfather's Journey*, 1993, and *The Rabbits*, 1998, a political fable by Shaun Tan and John Marsden. Apparently, there are few subjects that picture-books cannot handle if approached by artists who understand that much can be said through the relatively limited space available to them in this format.

A rich seam for contemporary illustrators to plunder is that of fairy tales; Trina Schart Hyman's *Rapunzel*, 1982, Fiona French's *Snow White in New York*, 1986, Paul O Zelinsky's *Rumpelstiltskin*, 1986, and Angela Barrett's *Snow White*, 1991, are superior examples of this genre. Of course there are many highlights in the realms of book illustration—Michael Foreman's understated and poetic etchings for Alan Garner's *The Stone Book Quartet*, 1976–1978, show a sensitive understanding of the texts they illustrate, for example—but some commentators have lamented the loss of illustration in contemporary children's books, particularly for older readers. Martin Salisbury points to "the Harry Potter effect", explaining that "the enormous success of JK Rowling's books has apparently led to age groups that would previously have expected to find pictures in their story books now regarding pictures as babyish".[15]

Above Illustration © 1982 Satoshi Kitamura, from *Angry Arthur*, written by Hiawyn Oram and illustrated by Satoshi Kitamura. Reprinted by permission of Anderson Press Ltd.
Overleaf Illustration © 1974 Michael Foreman, from *War and Peas*. Reprinted by permission of Anderson Press Ltd.

" Arthur's anger became a hurricane hurling rooftops and chimneys and church spires. "

Nonetheless, there are signs that the lavish illustration typical of Victorian literature is making a return. Philip Pullman took a step towards this with the sketches he provided for the opening of each chapter in *His Dark Materials* trilogy, 1995–2000, as well as his recent collaboration with John Lawrence in *Once Upon a Time in the North*. In recent years a number of profusely illustrated books for older readers have appeared and several writer-illustrator partnerships have evolved. Nick Sharratt has worked closely with Jacqueline Wilson ever since the publication of *Tracy Beaker*, 1991; Paul Stewart's *The Edge Chronicles* (from 1998) are rich in Chris Riddell's dynamic line drawings; and Tony DiTerlizzi's sketches and coloured prints complement Holly Black's verbal narrative in *The Spiderwick Chronicles* (from 2003). Sara Fanelli's *Pinnochio*, 2003, is a riot of playful collage and Lauren Child has imprinted her hotchpotch of light-hearted graphics onto Lindgren's *Pippi Longstocking*, 2007, but the mood of Paul Gallico's *The Snow Goose*, 2007, is echoed by Angela Barrett's wistful, sombre artwork. The acclaimed author David Almond has collaborated with Polly Dunbar on the poignant comedy, *My Dad's a Birdman*, 2007, and with Dave McKean on the altogether darker *The Savage*, 2008, which is stylistically reminiscent of graphic novels.

Original illustrations by John Lawrence from *Once Upon a Time in the North*, by Philip Pullman, illustrations © John Lawrence 2008, courtesy of the Seven Stories Collection.

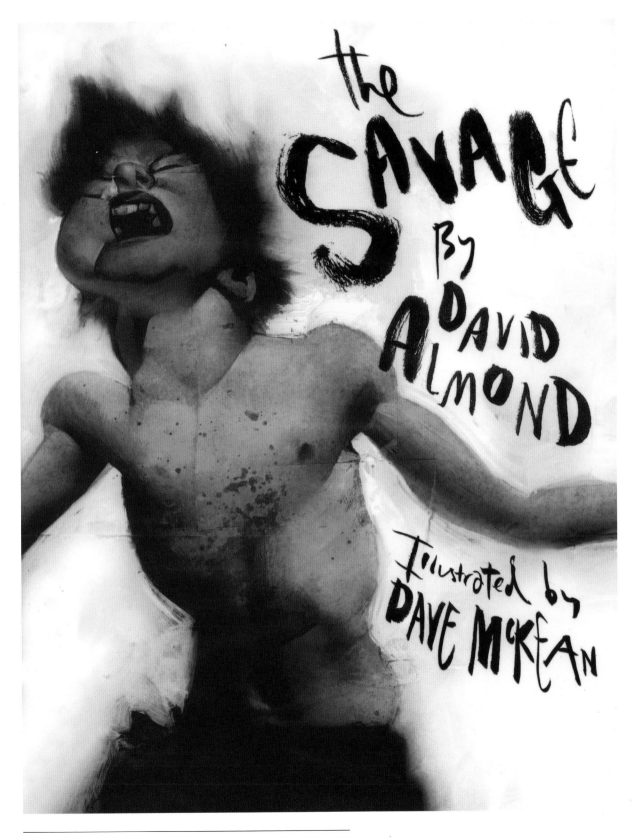

Illustration © 2008 Dave McKean, from *The Savage* by David Almond and illustrated by Dave McKean. Reproduced by permission of Walker Books Ltd, London SE11 5HJ.

Appointed children's laureate in 2009, Anthony Browne is an illustrator whose symbolic, multi-layered work is both creative and steeped in the history of children's book illustration. The influence of Dali and Magritte is evident in the direct intertextual references he makes to their artwork, for example in *Through the Magic Mirror*, 1976, and *Willy the Dreamer*, 1998, and Browne looks further back to Walter Crane, secreting Crane's iconic wolf in the forests of his own illustration, in his homage to fairy tales and the power of the imagination, *The Tunnel*, 1990. Browne is a practitioner who demonstrates that tradition is as important as innovation and that when we look forward to the future of children's publishing in the hands of new talents—Dave McKean, *The Wolves in the Walls* (with Neil Gaiman, 2003), and *The Day I Swapped My Dad for Two Goldfish*, 2004; Alexis Deacon, *Slow Loris*, 2003, and *Beegu*, 2004; Mini Grey, *The Adventures of the Dish and the Spoon*, 2007; Emily Gravett, *Meerkat Mail*, 2006, and *Spells*, 2008; Oliver Jeffers, *The Incredible Book Eating Boy*, 2006, and *The Great Paper Caper*, 2008, and Mo Willems, *Don't Let the Pigeon Drive the Bus*, 2003, and *Knuffle Bunny: A Cautionary Tale*, 2004; and Catherine Rayner, *Harris Finds His Feet*, 2008—we can't help but look back down the long history of book illustration, all the way back to John Amos Comenius and the shadows beyond, that has created the books we enjoy today.

Left Cover illustration © 2003 Alexis Deacon, from *Beegu*, by Alexis Deacon. Reprinted by permission of the Random House Group Ltd.
Right Cover illustration © 2002 Alexis Deacon, from *Slow Loris*, by Alexis Deacon. Reprinted by permission of the Random House Group Ltd.
Opposite *The Incredible Book Eating Boy* by Oliver Jeffers, text and illustrations © 2006 Oliver Jeffers. Reprinted by permission of HarperCollins Publishers Ltd.

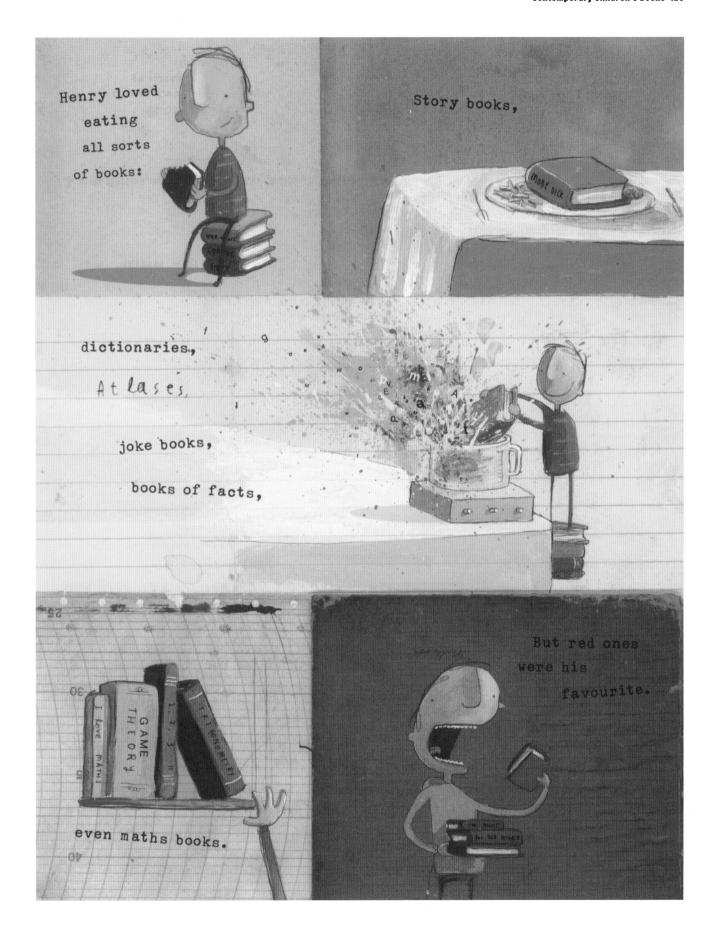

Henry loved eating all sorts of books:

Story books,

dictionaries,

At lases,

joke books,

books of facts,

even maths books.

But red ones were his favourite.

Illustrators and Authors 1945–Now

The Ahlbergs

Janet and Allan Ahlberg are one of the most successful author/illustrator collaborations of all time. Together they have produced 37 books for children, and one child.

They met when they were studying at teacher training college, and married in 1969. It was not until later, when Allan was working as a primary school teacher and Janet as a graphic designer, that she suggested he write a book that she could then illustrate. Allan was struck by the idea, and the two set about defining their style and inspirations. Initially their work was repeatedly rejected by many publishers, until one magical week when Penguin took on *The Old Joke Book*, A&C Black *The Vanishment of Thomas Tull* and Heinemann *Burglar Bill*; the Ahlbergs had taken off.

Allan has said that the books should always be viewed as a single entity with text and image working in unity, "a marriage of words and pictures". Their work often features folk or nursery rhyme characters and plots. Key influences are drawn from everyday surroundings, typical family life and their memories.

Each Peach Pear Plum, one of their most loved books which won Janet the Kate Greenaway Medal, is a peekaboo book in which recognisable children's favourites such as Tom Thumb, Mother Hubbard and the Three Bears hide amongst the illustrations. Another publication, *Peepo!*, shows the world from a baby's eyes as he watches the world around him, with circles cut out of each alternate page so that we can glimpse at what is to follow when we turn over the page. Janet's characters are often warm and rounded, with landscapes reminiscent of traditional Dutch and Flemish painting.

The Ahlbergs were typically experimental in their work and kept the edge on their creativity by varying the shape, style and functional qualities of their books. The hugely successful *The Jolly Postman* series is perhaps the best example of their innovative use of the physicality of a book's form. With a gently humorous rhyming narrative, the pages feature envelopes

Above and opposite bottom Illustrations © 2004 Jessica Ahlberg, from *Half a Pig*, written by Alan Ahlberg and illustrated by Jessica Ahlberg. Reproduced by permission of Walker Books Ltd, London SE11 5HJ.
Opposite top *Each Peach Pear Plum*, written by Alan Ahlberg and illustrated by Janet Ahlberg. © Janet and Alan Ahlberg 1977. Reproduced by permission of Penguin Books Ltd.

containing miniature letters addressed to fairy tale characters. Children can remove and handle the miniature letters, and so become involved in the plots in an entirely original and interactive way.

Sadly, Janet Ahlberg passed away in 1994, but Allan continues to write acclaimed children's books. He has currently authored over 140 titles which all share his warm and gentle sense of humour. His daughter Jessica now illustrates some of his books, such as *Half a Pig*, and the Ahlberg name remains a firm favourite amongst young readers.

ALL JOIN IN

Quentin Blake

Quentin Blake

Possibly the best known illustrator in Britain, Quentin Blake is an artist whose idiosyncratic, 'scribbly' style has made him a household name.

Blake's first illustrations were published by *Punch* magazine when he was just 16. He soon switched from political satire to book illustration, which allowed him to stretch his creativity, and where there was an abundance and variety of inspiration on every new page.

Blake illustrates using a light box, on which he places preliminary sketches drawn freely by hand. The initial drawing is then used as a starting point for a second production of the image, using dip pens or a vulture quill to develop the original (although not actually tracing it). Watercolour is then added. This allows for Blake's work to retain its spontaneity and for Blake to convey his desired style of movement, gesture and atmosphere.

Part of Blake's best known work is of course his illustrations for Roald Dahl. The first book Blake came to work on for Dahl was *The Enormous Crocodile* in 1975, and he continued to illustrate for him for the next 15 years until Dahl's death. One of the best-loved titles of the pair's collaboration is *The BFG*, and many believe Blake's image of the friendly giant is inspired by Dahl's own appearance. The relationship between Dahl's text and Blake's illustrations is so strong that they are practically now synonymous with one another.

Blake has illustrated for copious other esteemed writers from Russell Hoban to Michael Rosen on *Michael Rosen's Sad Book*, an incredibly moving and groundbreaking picture-book in which Rosen deals with the loss of his son. Blake illustrated the book with a sensitive precision; the last panel is simply left blank.

In addition, Blake is also an established author in his own right, with successful titles such as *Clown* and *All Join In* to his name. He maintains though, that he prefers to work visually.

Opposite Illustrations and text © 1990 Quentin Blake, from *All Join In* by Quentin Blake. Reprinted by permission of the Random House Group Ltd.
Above Illustrations © 1982 Quentin Blake, from *The BFG*, written by Road Dahl and illustrated by Quentin Blake. Reprinted by permission of AP Watt on behalf of Quentin Blake.
Overleaf *Michael Rosen's Sad Book*, illustrations © 2004 Quentin Blake. Reprinted by permission of AP Watt on behalf of Quentin Blake.

Anthony Browne

Anthony Browne's highly original style sets him apart from his contemporaries, and his strange illustrations, at the same time hyper-real and unreal, capture children's imaginations and invite them to explore the dream world that Browne so subtly creates.

Browne works in watercolour, and sometimes gouache, setting his work apart from the line drawings, or black line and block colour of many of his contemporaries and predecessors. Browne's admiration of the Surrealists, particularly Magritte, Dali and Rousseau, is evident in his work. Like Magritte, Browne is able to carefully fuse the surreal with the everyday to produce thought provoking illustrations, as shown in his precisely drawn but wildly imagined *Through the Magic Mirror*. His treatment of *Alice's Adventures in Wonderland*, 1988, introduces gorillas as players in the story, for example, Tweedledum and Tweedledee appear in gorilla form. His work is often witty, using visual or hidden jokes.

Despite the range of Browne's different characters, it is his gorillas for which he is best known, and which command the most immediate affection. A small series of books is based around Willy, a rather quiet, sensitive gorilla; through Willy we understand Browne's intrigue with gorillas as being both strong and gentle. *Willy the Wimp*, is about a small gorilla who takes up body-building to grow strong and stop others calling him a wimp; *Little Beauty*, 2008, is about a touching relationship between a gorilla and a small cat; *Gorilla*, is a magical tale about a toy gorilla who comes to life; in *Willy the Dreamer*, 1997, we see Willy dreaming that he is many things, with Browne's illustrations referring to his Surrealist heroes.

Browne's work brings together his technical skill as an illustrator, his love of the surreal and of Surrealist artists in particular to produce characters, tales and illustrations that are quiet, sensitive and often poignant. Browne works through often melancholy and challenging emotions via characters in his stories that are at once big and strong, as well as affectionate and wistful. His stories are faintly autobiographical; often using his own life events as a foundation, addressing various serious themes in his books.

Browne graduated from Leeds Art College with a graphic arts degree in 1967. He developed his high quality technical skill through three years as a medical illustrator at Leeds Royal Infirmary; he then spent 15 years illustrating greeting cards for Gordon Fraser. His first book was *Through the Magic Mirror*, 1976, but it was *Gorilla*, 1983, that first really cemented his reputation as an author/illustrator.

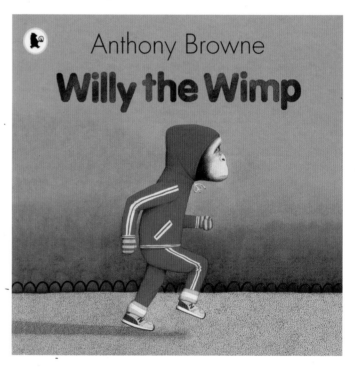

Above Cover illustration © 1984 Anthony Browne, from *Willy the Wimp* by Anthony Browne. Reproduced by permission of Walker Books Ltd, London SE11 5HJ.
Opposite and overleaf Illustrations © 1986 Anthony Browne, from *Piggybook* by Anthony Browne. Reproduced by permission of Walker Books Ltd, London SE11 5HJ.

Above and left Illustrations © 1983 Anthony Browne,
from *Gorilla* by Anthony Browne. Reproduced by permission of
Walker Books Ltd, London SE11 5HJ.
Opposite top and bottom Illustrations © 1976, 2000 Anthony
Browne, from *Through the Magic Mirror* by Anthony Browne.
Reproduced by permission of Walker Books Ltd, London SE11 5HJ.

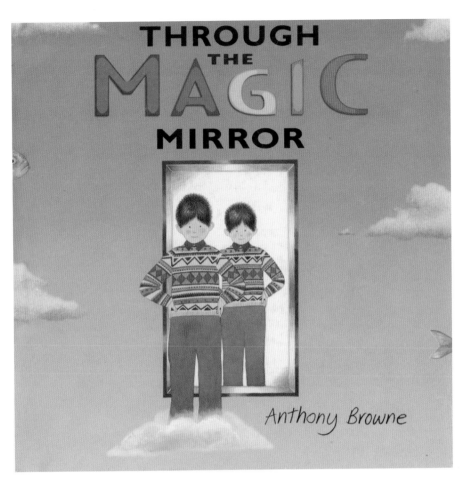

❝ Suddenly the sky became dark as a flock of choirboys flew overhead. ❞

Captain Pugwash
John Ryan

Captain Pugwash and his crew of motley pirates began life as a cartoon strip for *Eagle* magazine, before being adapted into a television series and immortalised in over 21 books.

The tales follow the escapades of the rather pompous Captain Pugwash as he attempts to rule the Seven Seas, but is usually hindered by his nemesis Cut-throat Jake; a considerably more accomplished pirate. Whenever Pugwash finds himself in a sticky corner, Tom the Cabin Boy saves the day and in truth is the real master of their ship, the Black Pig. The rest of the crew are rather crude figures of hilarity and highly comic in style, whilst

Tom is more realistically drawn and thus the link to reality and the reader.

The television series of the books was immensely popular, and the 86 five minute episodes were made by Ryan himself, and were first commissioned in 1957, with the latter shorts by Ryan being produced in 1975. He used a real-time animation technique where cutouts of the characters were moved across painted backgrounds with levers. The series was initially shot in black and white, but transferred into colour for the 1970s editions when Pugwash was at his peak of popularity.

New audiences were introduced to the clumsy Captain with a computer animated series, produced by John Carey films and with Ryan's approval in the late 1990s, allowing Pugwash to continue his adventures for a new generation.

John Ryan recently passed away, but he will be remembered for his witty style and great ability to create characters with a child-like innocence, whose success means they will remain household names for years to come.

Above and opposite *Pugwash and the Sea Monster*, text and illustrations © John Ryan 1976. First published by Frances Lincoln 2009.

"Sea Monster, heave to!" came a voice from inside the head.

" Splendid, me hearties! cried the Captain. "

Eric Carle

Eric Carle's *The Very Hungry Caterpillar* seems the simplest of stories, yet it has a powerful impact that remains right through to adulthood.

With its 'munched through' pages that encourage children to poke their fingers through the holes, and the endearing humpbacked, obsolete look of the caterpillar, the innovative and interactive page design is both playful and vibrant. Yet there is a subtext within the narrative that offers an educational tool, outlining not only the life cycle of a butterfly, but also teaching young readers the days of the week.

All of Eric Carle's books have an incredibly distinctive aesthetic which he achieves by building up his illustrations with tissue and acrylic paint, before photographing them for the actual book. The collages give the finished pictures a depth and finesse that define Carle's work, and make moments like the caterpillar's transformation into a butterfly truly beautiful. The book carries a message of hope, that even the ugliest little caterpillar can turn into the most stunning butterfly, yet there is also an underlying sadness in the transformation as something is lost that can never be re-found.

Eric Carle grew up in Nazi Germany, and he has said that his exuberant and joyful books are a rebellion against his own bleak childhood. He receives 10,000 fan letters every year from children all over the world and each new generation of young readers keep *The Very Hungry Caterpillar* in the bestsellers list.

Front cover illustration of *The Very Hungry Caterpillar* by Eric Carle (Hamish Hamilton 1970, Picture Puffins 1974, 2006). © Eric Carle, 1970. Reproduced by permission of Penguin Books Ltd.

Helen Craig

Illustrator of the famous *Angelina Ballerina* books, and author/illustrator of a wealth of other works, Helen Craig is one of the most successful figures in modern picture-books. She has written and/or illustrated over 60 publications—including over 20 in the Angelina series.

Unlike many of her contemporaries, Craig did not dream of becoming an artist when she was younger, and even though she loved drawing she did not seriously contemplate it as a profession until much later. She did however possess a great love of picture-books as a child, and would stare into the illustrations, willing them to come to life. At 16 she went to work as an apprentice at a photography firm and later set up her own studio in London.

It was not until 1969 that Craig started to illustrate children's books; one of her main inspirations was Maurice Sendak's *Where the Wild Things Are*, which she bought to read to her young son. The first book Craig illustrated was *Wishing Gold* by Robert Nye in 1970. She later explored the creative use of a books design with *The Mouse House ABC*, which was produced in the form of a concertina that fitted into a little slipcase, published in 1978.

Mice make regular appearances in much of Craig's work, largely because of their capabilities to mimic human postures and emotions. They can be drawn standing on their hind legs and have clearly defined hands and feet, and the added bonus of a tail, which Craig uses to help express emotion.

The most famous mouse in Craig's work is of course Angelina, and the joint venture between Craig and writer Katharine Holabird has been adapted into a television show with a new series starting in Autumn 2009, and a ballet aimed at children by the English National Ballet. Other mice found in Craig's work include Charlie and Tyler, who first appeared in her version of Aesop's Fable *The Town Mouse and the Country Mouse*, and were then revisited in *Charlie and Tyler at the Seaside*.

" One night Angelina even danced in her dreams, and when she woke up in the morning she knew that she was going to be a real ballerina some day. "

Craig works by sketching out her drawings and then painting over them in watercolour, with her initial shading and cross-hatching still visible underneath the colours. She has also experimented with etchings and aquatints, as shown in *The Yellow House*. She continues to produce exciting new titles, such as her collaboration with Philippa Pearce, *A Finder's Magic,* and there are two new Angelina books in the pipeline.

Opposite top Illustration © 1987 Helen Craig, from *The Yellow House*, written by Blake Morrison and illustrated by Helen Craig. Reproduced by permission of Walker Books Ltd, London SE11 5HJ.
Opposite bottom Illustration © 2008 Helen Craig, from *A Finder's Magic* written by Philippa Pearce and illustrated by Helen Craig. Reproduced by permission of Walker Books Ltd, London SE11 5HJ.
Above *Angelina Ballerina* © 1983 Helen Craig and Katharine Holabird.

Penguin bit Lion
very hard
on the nose.

OW! said Lion.

WOW! said Ben.

And Penguin said ...

Polly Dunbar

Polly Dunbar's first two books were published when she was just 16. She went on to study Illustration at Brighton University, and is now one of the most highly regarded young talents working in children's books today.

Her early works explored teenage issues relevant to her in *Help! I've Forgotten my Brain* and *Help! I'm Out with the In-crowd*. Her university projects included her *Hole Story* series, which re-tells the stories of Henry VIII, Cleopatra and Scrooge, but with holes cut out of the books to reveal the next steps of the narrative. After graduating, Dunbar worked on a series of projects for other writers, before returning to writing again for *Flyaway Katie*.

Flyaway Katie tells the story of a young girl who is feeling grey. Jealous of the brightly coloured, exotic birds in a picture on her wall at home, she decides to transform herself. She dresses up in a large green hat, yellow tights and paints her face blue, and then magically flies into the picture to spend the afternoon with the happy birds, before returning home for her bath. The book is a comment on colour's ability to change moods and art's ability to inspire imagination. Dunbar's exuberant illustrations capture children's amazement at the world around them.

Dunbar has since worked on other exciting titles such as *Dog Blue, Shoe Baby*—written by her mother, Joyce Dunbar, also a writer—and *My Dad's a Birdman*, written by David Almond. The story, set in the north of England, is shaped around "The Great Human Bird Competition", which the main character Lizzie's Dad is determined to win; he makes himself a pair of wings and sets about becoming the best bird possible. The book deals with serious issues such as death, mental illness and child carers, yet it remains a funny and heartfelt story of hope, trust and love. Dunbar's illustrations capture the light-heartedness of the book, and display her fine use of watercolour as well as seeing her experiment with collage for aspects of the illustrations, such as Lizzie's Dad's wings and nest. One of Dunbar's recent publications, *Penguin*, is a comic tale of a child wishing and believing a toy to be real, and Dunbar relates the tale with equal wit in both the text and the illustrations.

Polly Dunbar is also the co-founder of the Long Nose puppet company, which has adapted Dunbar's books into shows, including a new production of *Flyaway Katie*.

Opposite Illustrations © 2007 Polly Dunbar, from *Penguin*, written and illustrated by Polly Dunbar. Reproduced by permission of Walker Books Ltd, London SE11 5HJ.
Left Illustration © 2007 Polly Dunbar, from *My Dad's a Birdman*, written by David Almond and illustrated by Polly Dunbar. Reproduced by permission of Walker Books Ltd, London SE11 5HJ.

Sara Fanelli

Sara Fanelli stands out from her contemporaries through her roots in European art practices. She was born in Florence, but moved to London to study at Camberwell College of Art, where she produced her first published picture-book, *Button*.

Her style is highly personal and original, and Fanelli does not allow her work to be restrained or inhibited by typical expectations of how picture-books should be produced and understood. She uses a plethora of techniques to achieve her idiosyncratic illustrations, that blend amusing doodle-like sketches with a rich layering of collage, set against coloured backgrounds. The collages are comprised of anything from fabric, newspaper cuttings in various languages, pictures of Fanelli as a child, eyes cut from photographs and added to her characters; even scanned in images of pasta and sugar are used to add further texture and depth to the pages. She often adds price tags in currencies from days gone by, and old fashioned postage stamps, giving an archaic feel and linking her to the work of Duchamp and other Dadaists in her use of found objects and historical typefaces. Her collages allow her to interweave her narratives with elements from different times and place.

The drawings themselves, scribbly and child-like in style, are drawn over the collages. Fanelli focuses her compositions on line and shape, disregarding tone. *Dear Diary*, published in 2000, places her illustrations amongst stationary objects, with pages torn from exercise books and graph paper littering the narratives of the days of her different characters, including a girl, a chair, a knife and a fork, and Fanelli's own childhood dog, Buba. Fanelli's upbringing is often an inspiration to her, and there is a sense in her work that she has retained a part of her childhood self.

In 2003, Fanelli illustrated a new version of Carlo Collodi's *Pinocchio*, translated by Emma Rose. Her stick-like, black line figures are reminiscent of American graffiti artist Jean-Michel Basquiat, and once again Fanelli makes inventive use of her collection of old photographs and stationary. Her final image of Pinocchio as a "real boy" is an eighteenth century black and white photograph of a sombre looking child, but Fanelli has added the characteristics of her drawings for the character: a pointed hat, rosy cheeks, and of course, an elongated pointed nose.

Sara Fanelli has reshaped the way that picture-books can be formatted and created. Her playful style and unconventional use of collage have been influential to other emerging talents in illustration, and her various publications show that future picture-books can continue to break new ground in illustration and design.

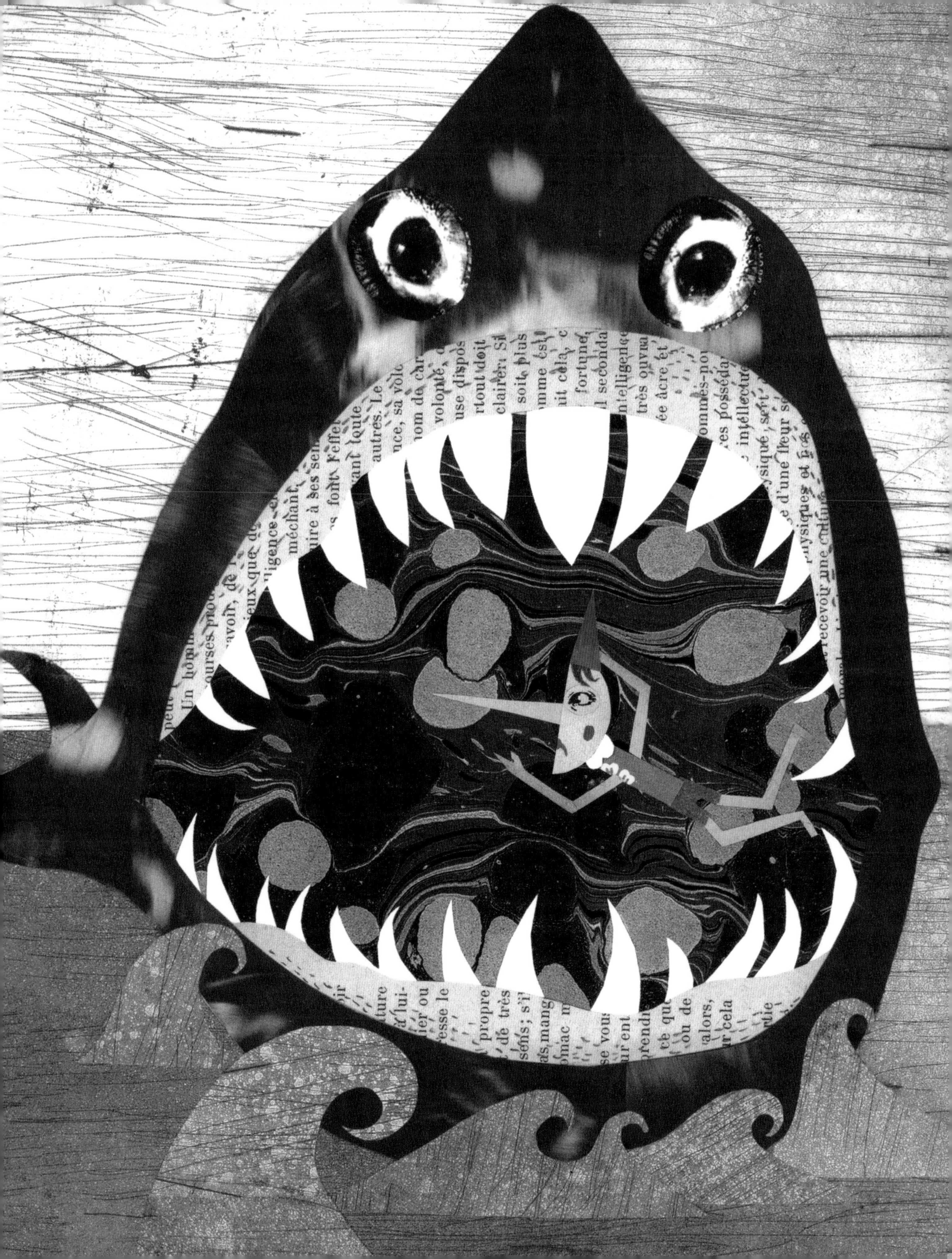

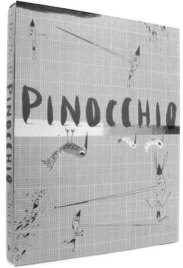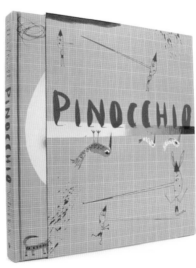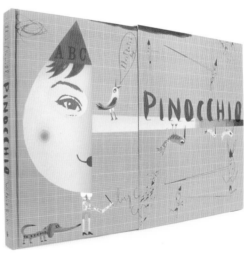

Top and opposite Illustrations © 2000 Sara Fanelli, from *Dear Diary*, written and illustrated by Sara Fanelli. Reproduced by permission of Walker Books Ltd, London SE11 5HJ.

Bottom Illustrations © 2003 Sara Fanelli, from *Pinocchio*, written by Carlo Collodi and illustrated by Sara Fanelli. Reproduced by permission of Walker Books Ltd, London SE11 5HJ.

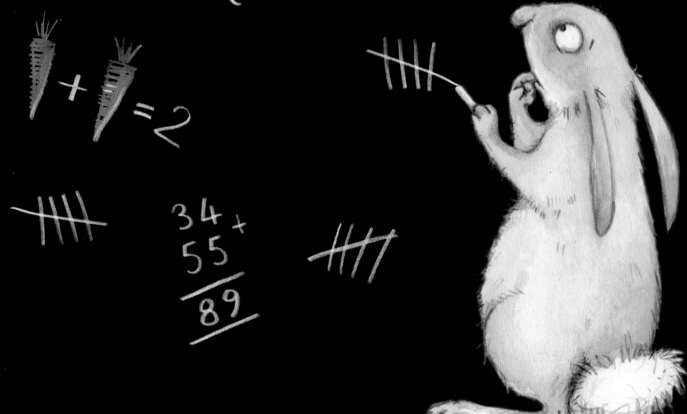

The Rabbit Problem

by

Emily Gravett

(and a lot of rabbits)

Emily Gravett

A truly exciting new illustrator, Emily Gravett beautifully combines detailed watercolour sketches with absorbing and inventive narratives to create picture-books that are nearly single-handedly driving the way for new talent in illustration.

Always keen to explore form and content, her first book, *Wolves*, follows a rabbit as he becomes increasingly engrossed in a library book about wolves, to the extent that he fails to notice the real wolf that is slowly stalking him. The book combines real facts about wolves and their habits which are interspersed into the narrative, as well as removable library tickets and overdue letters which help to create a sophisticated design that is juxtaposed with the deliberately clumsy representation of the rabbit himself. The book finishes with two surprise endings, which have since become a key trait in Gravett's books.

Gravett continued to experiment with form in her *Little Mouse's Big Book of Fears*; the pages of which are worn and torn to lend a 3-D effect to aspects of the illustrations. The wearing down of the pages was actually carried out by her daughter's rats, who obligingly nibbled on corners and even urinated on paper which was then scanned into the computer by Gravett, to help give an authentic feel. Each page of the book details a different fear of Little Mouse's, such as birds which make him "feel twitchy". This fear is illustrated by a roughly sketched owl accompanied by real feathers, scanned in and given facial expressions by Gravett, again juxtaposing the simplicity of the owl with the highly defined feathers. Mouse always carries an oversized pencil with him, symbolising the power of the pen and creative expression.

Spending eight years as a traveller and living in an old bus with her partner and daughter, Gravett only arrived at picture-book illustration after enrolling on an art foundation course when her partner brought her home a college prospectus. Within a week, she had found her calling and fought her way onto Brighton University's Illustration course, where she focused all of her projects around picture-books. This allowed her to develop her detailed and expressive style often achieved using pencil, crayon and watercolour, and to explore the effectiveness of collage, as demonstrated

in books such as *Spells* and *Meerkat Mail*—in part a testament to Gravett's travelling days.

Gravett strives to adhere to a two book per year work pattern, and her most recent offering *The Rabbit Problem* helps to cement her position as one of the most innovative author/illustrators at a time when picture-books are regarded by many to be in decline. Gravett proves that there is still huge talent out there that is capable of producing future classics. Gravett herself recognises the talent that exists in her work and her contemporaries, and believes that we could, in fact, be entering a golden age for illustration.

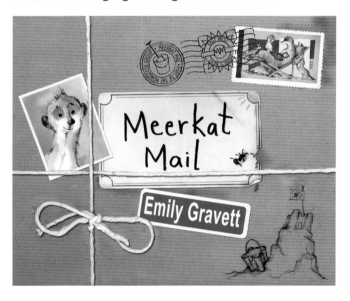

Opposite Text and illustrations © 2009 Emily Gravett, from *The Rabbit Problem* by Emily Gravett.
Above Text and illustrations © 2006 Emily Gravett, from *Meerkat Mail* by Emily Gravett.
Overleaf Text and illustrations © 2007 Emily Gravett, from *Little Mouses Big Book of Fears* by Emily Gravett.

Ablutophobia
(Fear of bathing)

Use the space below to record your fears.

Hydrophobia
(*Fear of water*)

Use the space below to record your fears.

Flushed down

the loo!

Mini Grey

Mini Grey is one of the most exciting new author/illustrators producing books today. Using computer technology as well as her vast imagination and drawing skills, Grey's work is utterly unique and impossible to pigeon-hole.

Her books often explore well-known stories or situations but from an entirely new viewpoint, such as in *The Pea and the Princess* and *The Adventures of the Dish and the Spoon*.

Arriving at illustration after work in varied fields from theatre carpentry, teaching and puppet making, Grey's first book was *Egg Drop*. It is a cautionary tale of an impatient egg who is determined to fly. Dreaming of joining the birds, aeroplanes and clouds high up in the sky, the Egg decides to climb a Very Tall Tower and steps off to join the high-flyers. Things of course, do not go quite to plan, and although the egg is rescued from the fall, it ends up on a plate, blissfully unaware of the nearby dangers of a knife and a fork.

Although *The Pea and the Princess* and *Traction Man* (an action figure who busies himself rescuing various items in a family's home) were both shortlisted for the Kate Greenaway Medal, it was *The Adventures of the Dish and the Spoon* which finally won it for Grey.

The story picks up where the nursery rhyme ends, and we follow the Dish and the Spoon as they journey to America, find fame and fortune, only to have the Dish while it all away in her pursuit of a glamorous lifestyle. The pair end up in jail after attempting to rob a bank to help them settle their debts, and although everything falls apart (the Dish literally), the story still ends happily. Reminiscent of 1940s Hollywood, and in its way comparable to *Citizen Kane*, Grey's imaginings of the famous Dish and Spoon's travels are dramatic, emotional, and cleverly humorous.

Grey uses a variety of the usual illustrator utensils of pens, pencils, watercolours and crayons, but also adds her own individual techniques that can see her use anything from bleach, household emulsion, aerosol car paint to coffee spills. She brings her great mass of material together via her computer, which allows her to experiment with different formats. She also uses a scanner to bring in real objects to her illustrations, as well as drawing and colouring by hand.

Mini Grey continues to push the boundaries of what a picture-book can comprise with her innovative use of computer technologies, sharp eye for detail and original storylines. She is an example of an author/illustrator who redefines the picture-book format and advances its evolvement for new generations of readers.

Left and above *Egg Drop* © Mini Grey 2002.
Opposite *Traction Man is Here* © Mini Grey 2005.

Traction Man is guarding some toast.

The Adventures of the Dish and the Spoon © Mini Grey 2006.

The Gruffalo
Julia Donaldson
and Axel Scheffler

The hugely successful author/illustrator partnership of Julia Donaldson and Axel Scheffler began back in 1993 with *A Squash and a Squeeze*, but their work together on *The Gruffalo* is by far their most famous.

The story is a modern-day verse fable, originally derived from a Chinese folk tale where a child cons a jungle tiger into submission after encouraging it to follow her footsteps. For *The Gruffalo*, Donaldson switched the tiger to an imaginary monster and the child to an astute mouse, who evades various animals of the forest by warning them that a terrible Gruffalo is meeting him "Here, by these rocks, And his favourite food is roasted fox", and so on. The plan serves him well, until he encounters a real Gruffalo and must use his cunning to stop being eaten himself.

Written in just two weeks, *The Gruffalo* was a massive success, which Donaldson has attributed to the fact that "all children like being scared and having that fear relieved. They feel empowered by that." Undoubtedly also key to its success were Scheffler's illustrations that capture the shrewdness of the mouse and the naivety of the Gruffalo with detailed precision.

Scheffler's Gruffalo is quite different to Donaldson's own initial imagining of the monster, which she saw as being alien-like and brightly coloured. However, Donaldson stood corrected when she first saw Scheffler's horned bovine-like representation of her character. The forest in the book is stripped of any evidence of human interference—no houses, no clothes, no furniture. Scheffler's early sketches for the book show the Gruffalo on all fours and the characters clothed, but Donaldson wanted a more naturalistic look, though the creatures have deliberately been given some human characteristics and mouse and the Gruffalo both walk on their hind legs.

The book has since been turned into a sell-out stage production and will be screened (at Christmas time) as

an animated television programme narrated by Helena Bonham Carter and with Robbie Coltrane as the voice of the Gruffalo. Donaldson and Scheffler also gave in to pressure and produced a sequel, *The Gruffalo's Child*. It sees the Gruffalo's daughter venturing out into the snowy forest to see if she can find the Big Bad Mouse her father has warned her about, but ends up running back home to the safety of their cave.

Donaldson and Scheffler have proved that they are a formidable picture-book duo, with each of their talents complementing the other's and contributing equally to a book's success. Donaldson has admitted that she often has Scheffler's illustration style in mind when she is writing.

> **❝ A gruffalo?**
> **What's a gruffalo?**
> **A gruffalo!**
> **Why, didn't you know? ❞**

" . . . Oh!"

But who is this creature with terrible claws
And terrible teeth in his terrible jaws?
He has knobbly knees and turned-out toes
And a poisonous wart at the end of his nose.
His eyes are orange, his tongue is black;
He has purple prickles all over his back.

"Oh help! Oh no!
It's a gruffalo!"

This page and opposite Illustrations from *Dogger* © 1977 Shirley
Hughes. Reproduced by permission of the artist.

Shirley Hughes

With her incredible talent for reproducing children's mannerisms, expressions and body language, Shirley Hughes' realistic approach to illustration has ensured her lasting appeal to readers of many ages.

Frequently armed with a sketchbook, Hughes' ability to observe and record people in their daily existence results in her books being full of characters whose warmth radiates off the page.

Capable of drawing nearly at the same speed as seeing, Hughes uses her preliminary sketches as a reference point for storyboards and completed illustrations. Typically Hughes uses pen and ink, then watercolour and gouache to produce her work. Her stories are derived from the everyday dramas of a child's world, such as losing a favourite toy or having to finally let go of a much-loved security blanket.

The breakthrough book for Hughes that saw her advance into a global market was *Dogger*. Although set around that most English of events, a school sports day, the famous tale of security and sisterly kindness is easily related to audiences anywhere. Dogger's cocked ear made him an instantly lovable character and any child can feel Dave's pain at losing his favourite toy. In the end, it is Dave's sister Bella whose act of selflessness allows Dogger to find his way back into Dave's arms.

Further works of Hughes have helped to cement her reputation as one of the pioneers of realism in picture-books. Her *Alfie* series tells the everyday encounters of four year old Alfie and his little sister Annie Rose, neither of whom have aged physically, nor become dated, since the first book was released in 1981.

The *Lucy and Tom* series achieved similar success, the first of which, *Lucy and Tom's Day* was Hughes' first picture-book. The book was written in 1960 when there were many technical limitations with printing methods. Each colour would have to be separately produced and individually overlaid onto the image —a laborious process.

The draft illustrations for *Lucy and Tom's Day* show Hughes' beautiful use of watercolour to represent shadow and light, and her preliminary sketchy representations of Lucy and Tom reflect the innocence and simplicity of their life at home. Later *Lucy and Tom* books such as *Lucy and Tom Go to School* show the progression of Hughes' style, as well as that of new printing processes.

Hughes has spoken of the decline of picture-books, especially those for older readers but is confident in the power of illustration.

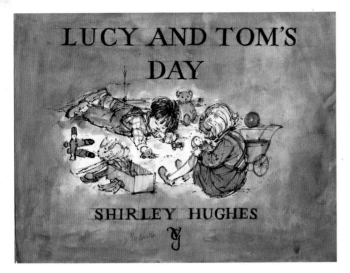

After tea is over they get out their toys and play.

After breakfast Lucy is very busy helping her mother about the house.
Tom especially enjoys making the beds.

Opposite Illustrations from *Alfie Gets in First* © 1981 Shirley Hughes. Reproduced by permission of the artist.
Above and overleaf Original artwork, courtesy of the Seven Stories Collection, from *Lucy and Tom's Day* © 1960 Shirley Hughes. Reproduced by permission of the artist.

Pat and Laurence Hutchins

Pat Hutchins' first picture-book was *Rosie's Walk*, which follows Rosie the Hen as she strolls around the farm, unaware that a fox is creeping behind her. The book was a great success.

As her career progressed Hutchins realised she was more comfortable writing than illustrating, and she and husband Laurence began collaborating on publications that she would write and he would illustrate, becoming a successful picture-book duo.

Before this success Hutchins faced repeated rejections from London publishing houses when she approached them for illustration jobs. When work took Laurence to New York, Pat moved with him, and decided to try her luck with publishers there. She had a warmer reception, and one editor liked a particular line in a book about farmyard noises, "This is the fox. He never makes a noise." Hutchins went away and even though she was yet unconvinced of her talents as a writer, started work on what would become *Rosie's Walk*.

At the time the book was published, full-colour printing was a rare practice due to high costs and Hutchins was asked to pre-separate her artwork, overlaying each illustration with each different colour. Hutchins was restricted to three colours, and chose red, yellow and black, producing other tones and colours by mixing this basic palette. After more than a year of experimentation, countless rewrites and hard work, the seemingly effortless book was finished. Hutchins' endeavours were rewarded and the book became an instant classic.

Since then Hutchins has continued to produce fresh and funny picture-books, and frequently collaborated with Laurence, who sadly died in 2008. Pat and Laurence often produced books about family life, sometimes featuring their own children, such as

Rosie's Walk, © 1968 Pat Hutchins, © renewed 1996 Pat Hutchins. Reprinted by permission of The Random House Group Ltd.

" Rosie the hen went for walk
across the yard
around the pond
over the haycock
past the mill
through the fence
under the beehives
and got back in time for dinner. "

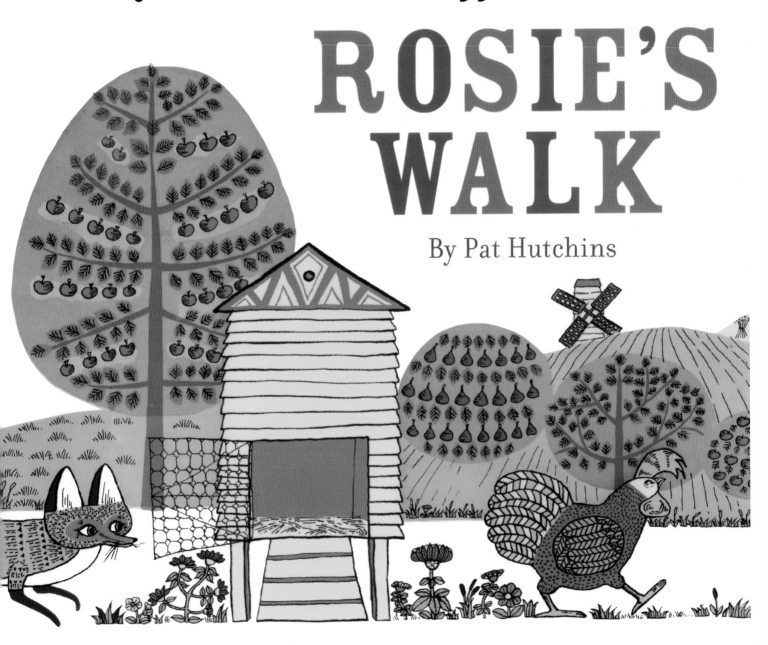

ROSIE'S WALK

By Pat Hutchins

The House that Sailed Away, which stars their son Morgan and features the rest of the family. The story tells of Grandma's visit over a very rainy weekend, which is so wet that the house actually sails away and they all embark on a wild adventure. One of Pat's vibrant family tales is *Tidy Titch*, published in 1971, which tells the story of young Titch whose room is always impeccably tidy, until Titch helps his older brother and sister to clean out their rooms, and in the process manages to cram his own with their cast-off toys.

Other works include a counting book for younger readers, *1 Hunter* from 1982, where the hunter believes himself to be alone in the jungle, but is actually surrounded by two elephants, three giraffes, four ostriches and so on. Her amusing characterisations, simple colour palette and detailed patterns are easily distinguishable and have marked Hutchins as an original and recognisable creator of children's books.

Previous pages Illustrations © 1975 Laurence Hutchins, from *The House that Sailed Away*, written by Pat Hutchins and illustrated by Laurence Hutchins. Original artwork courtesy of the Seven Stories Collection.

Above and overleaf Illustrations © 1971 Pat Hutchins, from *Tidy Titch*, by Pat Hutchins. Original artwork courtesy of the Seven Stories Collection.

30

31

Ezra Jack Keats

One of the most celebrated American authors and illustrators of the twentieth century, Ezra Jack Keats broke the colour barrier in mainstream children's book publishing in 1962, with his Caldecott Award-winning book *The Snowy Day*.

The beauty of Keats' achievement, the inclusion of children of many ethnic and racial groups, was made even more striking because it appeared to happen effortlessly, as if these books, about these children, had always been there.

His first picture book, *My Dog is Lost*, 1960, featured Juanito, a young boy newly moved to New York from Puerto Rico. Jaunito wanders the avenues of the complicated metropolis looking for his lost dog. During his journey he is joined by children of every sort, all dedicated to helping him find his dog.

Now she'll never come to my party,
thought Peter.
He saw his reflection in the street.
It looked all mixed up.

It was after *My Dog is Lost* that Keats went on to produce his classic series of books, a series that started with *The Snowy Day*. Keats' now beloved books focus on Peter, a young black boy whose creation was inspired by a photo Keats had seen in a copy of *Life* magazine 20 years earlier. It was a photo he had kept pinned to his studio wall without knowing why until he created Peter.

Opposite and above *A Letter to Amy*, © Ezra Jack Keats, 1968. Reproduced with special permission from the Ezra Jack Keats Foundation.

Whistle for Willie, © Ezra Jack Keats, 1964. Reproduced with special permission from the Ezra Jack Keats Foundation.

and up . . .
and down . . .
and around
and around.

In the 23 books that followed *The Snowy Day*, Peter was joined by his friends Roberto, Archie, Amy, Louie, his sister Suzie and his dog Willie. Each book focuses on a different child and a different adventure, always taking place in the same urban neighbourhood Keats based on his own childhood home.

Born Jacob Ezra Katz to a poor Polish immigrant family in 1916, Keats' ability as an artist was evident from a very young age. He frequently won competitions and awards and although he was offered three art school scholarships, Keats chose to stay at home in New York to help support his struggling family. After serving in the US Army during the Second World War, Keats worked in various jobs related to the arts and travelled to Europe to study painting in Paris.

After returning to New York, Keats had his first work exhibited at the Associated American Artists Gallery and consequently was commissioned to create the cover art for books by major publishers. It was at this time that he began working with Elisabeth Hubbard on the cover art for the book *Jubilant for Sure.* But in order to get more of this kind of work it became clear that Jacob Ezra Katz would have to become Ezra Jack Keats. This reality was a sad result of the anti-Semitic attitudes still prevalent at the time.

Keats himself has said "I didn't even ask to get into picture-books", but he slipped with ease into the industry, first creating illustrations for magazines, cover art for books, illustrating books written by others and finally writing and illustrating his own books for children. Following this path led him to revolutionise the world of American illustrated children's literature, creating books beloved by families all over the world.

Keats' illustration style is highly original, blending gouache paints (watercolour mixed with gum) with collages of his characters and props. Keats is perhaps best known for his pioneering use of collage, establishing it as a form often turned to by subsequent children's book illustrators. Through this approach he effectively recreates the back streets of New York, showing the dilapidation alongside the beauty that children will always see in the world they call home. In fact, Keats was the first children's book author to write tales set in a rundown urban environment rather than in an idyllic setting. The joy in his books is in his innocent portrayal of family life and the simple universal pleasures found in children's daily routines. When Keats died he left the royalties of his books to the foundation he had created that bears his name. In this way, his books continue to benefit children by helping to fund literacy and arts programmes in public schools, public libraries, museums, parks and universities across the United States.

Opposite *A Letter to Amy*, © Ezra Jack Keats, 1968. Reproduced with special permission from the Ezra Jack Keats Foundation.
Below *The Snowy Day*, © Ezra Jack Keats, 1962. Reproduced with special permission from the Ezra Jack Keats Foundation.

Above, opposite top and bottom, and overleaf Original artwork,
courtesy of the Seven Stories Collection, from *Mog the Forgetful Cat*
by Judith Kerr. © Kerr-Kneale Productions 1970.

Judith Kerr

Judith Kerr's highly acclaimed *Mog* series is a testament to her great love of cats, coupled with her determination to produce picture-books with simple but engaging language and story-lines.

In writing and illustrating her stories, Kerr wanted children to enjoy the process of learning to read. The *Mog* series, comprising 16 titles, ran from *Mog the Forgetful Cat* in 1970, where we are told that "Mog was nice but not very clever", to the moving *Goodbye Mog* of 2002.

Over her remarkable 30 year lifespan, Mog taught children across the globe to read, but also to love her endearing tabby features, animated expressions and innocent view of the world. Although Mog is not the brightest of cats, she always manages to save the day, whether it's alerting her family to burglars, saving babies or literally 'flying in' and winning pet competitions. With her tubby physique and satisfied grin, Mog is the perfect domestic cat. Kerr's publishers were apprehensive about *Goodbye Mog*, in which the famous kitty finally passed away. Kerr, however, insisted on the importance of introducing children to loss. The brave move pulled off, and *Goodbye Mog* was a huge success, becoming one of Kerr's best selling titles.

As an artist, Kerr herself has joked that she cannot draw tigers, "Look at the tiger in *The Tiger Who Came to Tea*, it's not a tiger at all." However, children still delighted in the tale of the tiger who turns a restricted, adult controlled world on its head when it arrives at Sophie's house and devours all the food and drink in sight. The tiger itself is striking in appearance; its finely detailed stripes and huge presence contrasting with the simplicity with which Kerr draws Sophie and her mother. There is also something slightly off kilter with the tiger, perhaps in his sly grin or his rigid posture at the table and the style with which he is drawn reflects the surreal quality of the book as a whole. Sophie still finds immense pleasure in the tiger's arrival, gently stroking his tail as he laps up all the water in the house.

Kerr's distinctive style not only captures a strong sense of the home and family, it effectively conveys emotion and, wherever possible, humour. Stretching herself from books for older readers, namely the *Out of the Hitler Time* trilogy, which draw on Kerr's own experiences of fleeing Nazi Germany as a young girl, to other picture-books including *Goose in a Hole* and the recent *One Night in the Zoo*, the beauty of Kerr's books and illustrations are in their humanity and warmth, and it is these which account for their enduring popularity.

Above and opposite Original artwork, courtesy of the Seven Stories Collection, from *The Tiger that came to Tea* by Judith Kerr. © Kerr-Kneale Productions 1968.

David McKee

Responsible for creating two very famous characters for at least two different generations of children, David McKee's books are likely to have a place on most children's bookshelves.

Mr Benn was his first successful creation, who was quickly turned into a series of just 13 episodes which then ran for the next 34 years. His second invention was *Elmer*, and the subsequent books have retained their initial popularity over the past 20 years. *Elmer the Patchwork Elephant* carries the message that it is fine to be different, and the 15 titles that followed the first publication have dealt with various moral and political topics, including *Elmer and the Hippos* which deals with issues surrounding immigration.

McKee has a firm background in fine art and is still a keen painter. His in-depth knowledge of art practices and love of artists from Paul Klee to Louis Vivin to Henri Matisse has influenced his style over the years, and much of his picture-book illustrations possess some of the qualities of early Modern art such as Cubism. Although no two books are the same,

McKee often uses lush highly-detailed backgrounds coupled with simple, line drawn characters as well as strange, angular perspectives. His perspective style developed after he sat on the floor reading to his three children, who although sitting at different angles to the picture, still understood it perfectly, leading McKee to the realisation that he could draw characters from different directions simultaneously.

Charlotte's Piggy Bank wonderfully demonstrates McKee's playful perspectives; with the characters and setting depicted as if from a bird's-eye view, yet still fully visible. Every person in the busy street scenes that provide the backdrop for the narrative has their own story, which can be followed alongside the main storyline of Charlotte and her new piggy bank. McKee believes that all illustrators are voyeurs, and his drawings are dotted with people watching from the sidelines or hidden behind curtains.

Tusk, Tusk, McKee's first picture-book is a tolerance tale about two tribes of black and white elephants, whose hatred of each other nearly drives them both to extinction, until a new tribe of grey elephants begin to appear; an early example of McKee's desire to bring moral twists to his children's books.

Not Now, Bernard was placed on the national curriculum and is a dark but humorous tale of Bernard whose life is taken over by a monster, but whose busy parents fail to even notice the switch. McKee's books often have a sharp, abrupt and ironic ending that twists how we understand picture-books, yet they remain immensely popular and continue to delight children of new generations.

Left *Tusk Tusk*, text and illustrations © David McKee. Reproduced by permission of Anderson Press Ltd.
Opposite *Not Now Bernard*, text and illustrations © David McKee. Reproduced by permission of Anderson Press Ltd.

NOT NOW, BERNARD

David McKee

Once, all the elephants in the world were black   or white. They loved all creatures,

One night Elmer couldn't sleep for thinking, and the think that he was thinking was that he was tired of being different. "Whoever heard of a patchwork elephant?" he thought. "No wonder they laugh at me."

In the morning before the others were really awake, Elmer slipped quietly away, unnoticed.

Top *Tusk Tusk*, text and illustrations © David McKee.
Reproduced by permission of Anderson Press Ltd.
Bottom *Elmer*, text and illustrations © David McKee.
Reproduced by permission of Anderson Press Ltd.

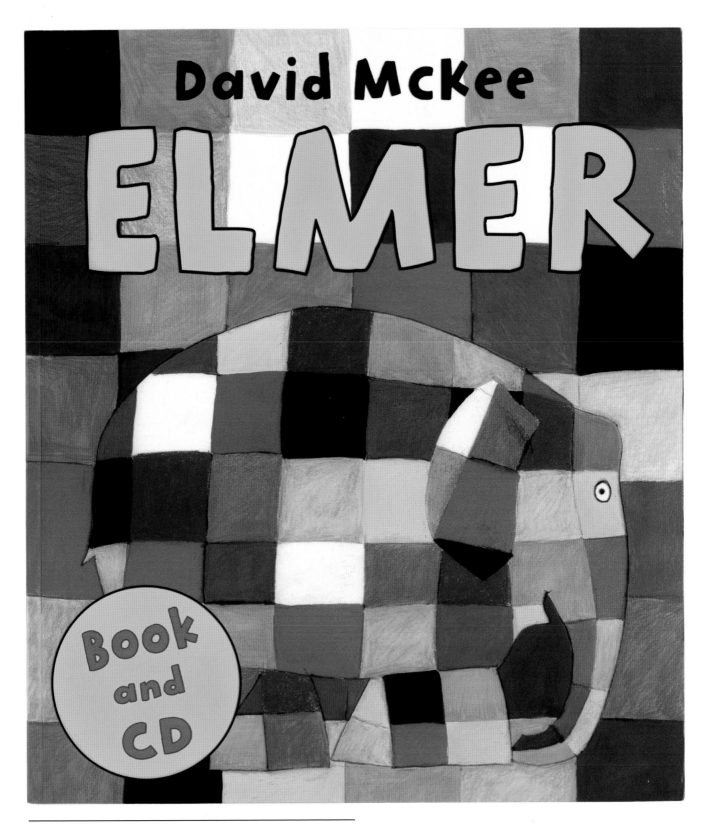

Above *Elmer*, text and illustrations © David McKee.
Reproduced by permission of Anderson Press Ltd.
Overleaf *Charlotte's Piggy Bank*, text and illustrations © David
McKee. Reproduced by permission of Anderson Press Ltd.

"I wish you were a flying pig,"
said Charlotte.
"That's it," said the pig and
there was a flash. There stood
the pig, only bigger and with wings.
"That's not fair, you tricked me,"
said Charlotte. "Where's my wish?
Where's my money?"

Above Illustrations © Mercis bv 1953–2009, from *Miffy* by Dick Bruna.
Opposite Illustrations © Mercis bv 1953–2009, from *Miffy at the Gallery* by Dick Bruna.

Miffy
Dick Bruna

The Miffy brand is one of the most internationally recognised and celebrated in children's books. Starting life as a fictional rabbit who lived in the garden of a holiday home, and invented to entertain Dick Bruna's son, Miffy was later developed into a book and became a girl purely because Bruna preferred drawing skirts to trousers.

Dick Bruna, Miffy's creator, was disillusioned by school at the end of the Second World War, and left his educational studies in order to join the family publishing business. It was whilst training in London that he first saw the work of the great artists such as Picasso and Matisse, and from then knew that art was his calling. Bruna paid homage to these influences in *Miffy at the Gallery*. His consequent background as a graphic artist gave him the firm belief that simplicity is the key to successful design and the creation of meaning; that by reducing everything to its essence and leaving out the unnecessary, children are free to let their imaginations roam. Bruna puts Miffy's fame down to the simplicity with which her friends and herself are drawn.

Miffy is always drawn using the same four basic colours of red, yellow, green and blue and the consistency of shape for the various characters is also key, meaning that everything is always clear and easily recognisable to young readers. Each image is outlined with a black contour, which Bruna paints on by hand, resulting in a slightly jagged edge. Although Bruna has been painting Miffy for over 50 years, it can still take him 100 sketches to produce a new picture of her. The *Miffy* books are 15.5cm by 15.5cm to make them manageable for small hands and they are nearly always comprised of 12 illustrations, each with four accompanying lines of text set out in alternate rhyme.

Then she found some paper
and made a picture.

At the end of the day,
Miffy put all her pictures up on the wall.

'That looks wonderful, Miffy,'
said Mother Bunny.
'It's your very own gallery.'

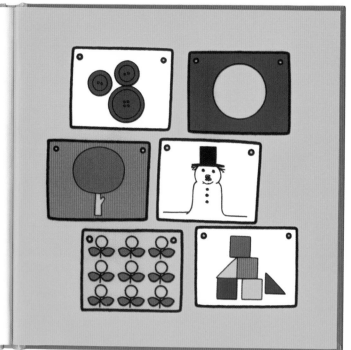

Above Illustrations © Mercis bv 1953–2009, from *Miffy the Artist*
by Dick Bruna.
Opposite Illustrations © Mercis bv 1953–2009,
from *Miffy's Dream* by Dick Bruna.

The *Miffy* series is aimed at two to six year olds, and Miffy herself seems to change her behaviour between that of a baby and a five year old depending on the content of each book. The first book in the series, *Miffy*, published in 1955, tells the story of Mr and Mrs Bunny who have a baby, called Miffy, and all the animals on the farm come to pay her a visit. In the early editions of the book Miffy looked more like a toy rabbit than she does today, but she has remained mostly the same since 1963 and Bruna reproduced the original books to fit the new vision of Miffy.

Although the illustrations are plain and uncomplicated, Bruna manages to convey emotions and expressions with the slightest brush stroke, and publications such as *Dear Grandma Bunny*, where Miffy deals with her grandmother's death, are incredibly moving for children. However, the books generally have happy endings, and children delight in the friendly stories which see Miffy and her friends have small, easy, everyday adventures.

The Miffy character has been used to raise funds that will enable libraries to be built in developing countries. She has also undertaken a world tour, visiting schools, hospitals and libraries, where she has drawn crowds of eager children from all cultures. She is truly an internationally iconic image, and with Bruna himself deeply committed to fundraising causes supported by his creation, she is testament to this artist's belief that images that are straightforward and simple can deliver the most powerful messages of all.

Right Illustrations © Mercis 1953–2009, from *Dear Grandma Bunny*, by Dick Bruna.
Opposite Illustration © Mercis bv 1953–2009, from *Miffy's Dream* by Dick Bruna.

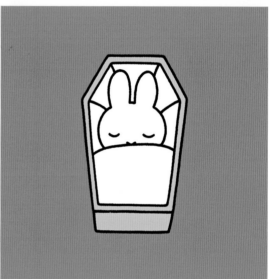

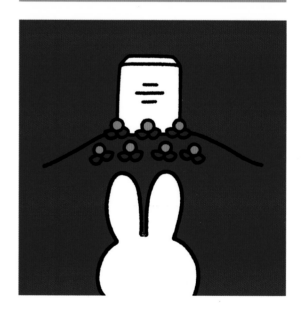

Quick! Back through the cave! Tiptoe! Tiptoe! Tiptoe!

Back through the snowstorm! Hoooo wooooo! Hoooo wooooo!

Back through the forest! Stumble trip! Stumble trip! Stumble trip!

Back through the mud! Squelch squerch! Squelch squerch!

Back through the river! Splash splosh! Splash splosh! Splash splosh!

Back through the grass! Swishy swashy! Swishy swashy!

Helen Oxenbury

Helen Oxenbury is known for her development of the baby board book, as well as her varied work for writers including Michael Rosen and Trish Cooke.

Growing up during the Second World War, picture-books were a rarity in Oxenbury's childhood, although she always possessed a great love of drawing. After attending art school, she completed a course in costume design, although her teacher advised her to switch to illustration as she was always most interested in character. Her early career saw her working on set and scenery design for theatre, film and television.

It was not until she met and married esteemed illustrator John Burningham that Oxenbury began to consider illustration as a career. She learned a great deal from him, and has likened his influence to that of a teacher or illustration course. After their first baby was born, Oxenbury started to produce her baby board books, an innovation at a time when books targeted at babies were almost unheard of. The books encouraged babies to engage with recognisable occurrences from their daily routines, and the babies were drawn with a soft simplicity of line and painted in watercolour. Her later 'Big Baby' board books for toddlers progressed to slightly older issues, with the babies painted in gouache with bold primary colours.

Both Oxenbury and Burningham were a part of the cultural changes of the 1960s that saw picture-book illustration open up to include a wealth of new styles, techniques and subject matter that allowed illustrators to express themselves with a freedom that had previously been inhibited. Illustration became less rigid and held less emphasis on the importance of realism, so picture-books began to play with perspective, drawings styles mimicked that of a child's own and creativity was opened up to include different techniques such as collage.

In 1989, Oxenbury collaborated with previous children's laureate Michael Rosen on *We're Going on a Bear Hunt*. The book tells the story of three young siblings on a day out with their elder brother, who all embark on a journey across the countryside in search of a bear. The rhythmic repetition and onomatopoeic style of the text means it is easily read aloud and memorised by children. The song itself does not actually state who is partaking in the hunt, and Rosen originally envisioned a line of Kings and Queens on a hunting expedition. Oxenbury instead sent the family on the trip, and her illustrations work by a page of black and white pencil sketches whilst they decide what to do, followed by a burst of watercolour for when they are journeying through the landscapes. The accompanying dog adds some subtle humour, and the end illustration of the bear dejectedly walking along the lonely beach is wittily ironic, yet also touching.

Later working with other writers such as Trish Cooke on *So Much*—who presented Playdays for nine years and has also written for *The Tweenies* and a number of plays—Oxenbury continued to represent familial bonds with her joyful illustrations.

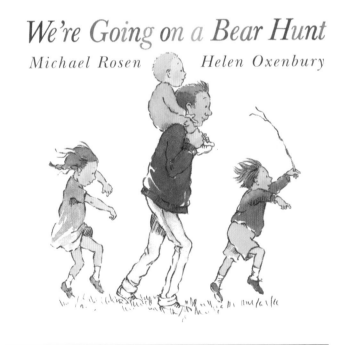

Opposite and above Illustrations © 1989 Helen Oxenbury, from *We're Going on a Bear Hunt*, written by Michael Rosen and illustrated by Helen Oxenbury. Reproduced by permission of Walker Books Ltd, London SE11 5HJ.

So Much!

TRISH COOKE   HELEN OXENBURY

The book is seen from the point of view of a baby who is greeted by members of his extended family as they arrive for his Daddy's surprise birthday party. The book is a celebration of family love and the baby's pleasure in feeling loved "so much" is captured in Oxenbury's vibrant colours and ink illustrations.

Oxenbury won the Kate Greenaway Medal for her modern take on *Alice in Wonderland*; Alice is transformed into a modern girl of our time, with contemporary clothes and a modern child's confidence, rather than the traditional Alice's rather Victorian attitude. Oxenbury is aware of how visually literate children are today, and the need for them to identify with the characters they see. She believes that by understanding the illustrations, the words become less daunting and encourage children to approach reading with greater confidence.

Opposite, below and overleaf Illustrations © 1994 Helen Oxenbury, from *So Much*, written by Trish Cooke and illustrated by Helen Oxenbury. Reproduced by permission of Walker Books Ltd, London SE11 5HJ.

Jan Pieńkowski

With a huge variety of achievements to his name—from pioneering the modern day pop-up book, illustrating the hugely successful Meg and Mog series and channelling the beauty of traditional fairy tale illustrations with his trademark silhouetted figures—Jan Pieńkowski is a prolific illustrator whose influence is felt across many different picture-book formats.

Pieńkowski grew up in Nazi occupied Poland, and his Eastern European routes often translate into his illustrations. One of his earliest works, *The Kingdom Under The Sea* (written by Joan Aiken) was a re-telling of Eastern European folk tales; the illustrations largely created from Pieńkowski's memories of the dense forests and small towns that he grew up around.

The use of silhouetted imagery is inspired by Polish traditions of paper cutting that Pieńkowski also remembers from his childhood. This signature style however was actually the result of a happy mistake. Pieńkowski was submitting a sample image to a potential publisher, but not satisfied with the expressions of the characters, decided to ink them in. When the drawings were accepted, Pieńkowski developed this style and subsequently produced more beautifully crafted silhouettes against striking backgrounds in books such as *A Necklace of Raindrops*.

Pieńkowski studied at King's College, Cambridge, where he became involved with stage sets and poster design. He went on to co-found the Gallery Five Company which amongst other things produced gift cards, which gave birth to the beginnings of Pieńkowski's pop-up creations. Truly original and highly inventive, pop-up books such as *Little Monsters*, and especially *Haunted House*, amused their readers with entirely new methods of engagement.

Many people will know Pieńkowski for his collaboration with writer Helen Nicoll and their *Meg and Mog* series. The darkly comic stories and vivid illustrations have ensured the continuing success of *Meg and Mog*, as have the books' creative design and format. With a set colour palette and bold, multiple contrasting colours appearing on different pages, no two pages of the same book use the same shade. Nicoll and Pieńkowski work fantastically well together and have done for the past 35 years.

Above Illustration from *The Kingdom Under The Sea*
© Jan Pieńkowski 1971.
Opposite Illustration from *A Necklace of Raindrops*
© Jan Pieńkowski 1968.

They went out in a boat

Meg at Sea © Helen Nicoll and Jan Pieńkowski 1973.

big cake
little bun

Pieńkowski's signature colours develop into the *Nursery Books*.
Sizes explores the relationship between big and small, adult and
child, as well presenting a child's view of the world around them.
Targeted at nursery age children, it is a simple but witty book that
contrasts the great and the small. © Jan Pieńkowski 1973.

Neither the text nor the image presides over the other, and often Nicoll will adjust the text to fit with the illustrations, and vice versa.

By his own admission, Pieńkowski is "not a born draughtsman", but the beauty of his illustrations lie in his use of colour, composition and his ability to depict the flow of movement. In a recent publication *The Thousand Nights and One Night* (a retelling of *The Arabian Nights* by David Walser), the characters leap across the pages with an energy that sweeps the reader up like a magic carpet. Many of the backgrounds against which the silhouettes are placed are from images Pieńkowski took at the Science Museum in London, and are tiny molecular structures of various metals and minerals, which are then scanned into the computer and blended with the illustrations using Photoshop.

Pieńkowski is currently working on an abridged version of the Old Testament, an introduction to the Bible stories for young readers entitled *In the Beginning*. The book is illustrated in the same style as *Meg and Mog* and promises to be a playful retelling of the great tales, and will add another classic title to Pieńkowski's varied body of work.

This page and opposite Illustrations from *The Thousand Nights and One Night* © Jan Pieńkowski 2007.

Richard Scarry

Richard Scarry started his life as a writer/illustrator at Little Golden Books, and published a huge wealth of work with them over their 20 year working relationship. Little Golden Books was established with the intention of making books accessible to all children, not just the upper classes and each book printed by the company cost just 25 cents.

Little Golden Books changed the history of publishing and how we consume literature, and Richard Scarry was an important figure amongst their original writing team. He later moved to Random House, but his use of animal characters, (including Mr Frumble, Huckle Cat and Mr Fixit) and narratives comprising information about various vocations, locations and everyday matters, remained the same.

Scarry once said, "I'm not interested in creating a book that is read once and then placed on the shelf and forgotten", and his rich layering of detail and action ensures that children find new excitement with multiple readings of a book. His contribution to children's literacy and development of their understanding of the world around them marks him as an important figure in the history of picture-books.

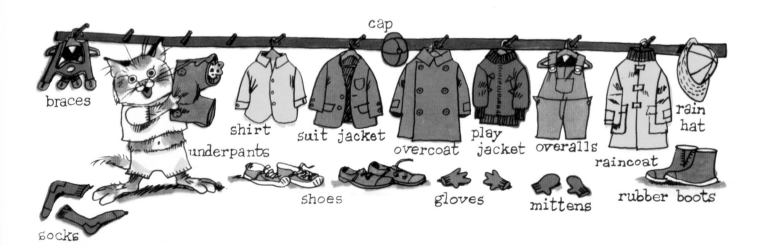

Soon it is crossing the wide ocean.
There is no land in sight.
Just look at all the things that
happen on an ocean-going ship!

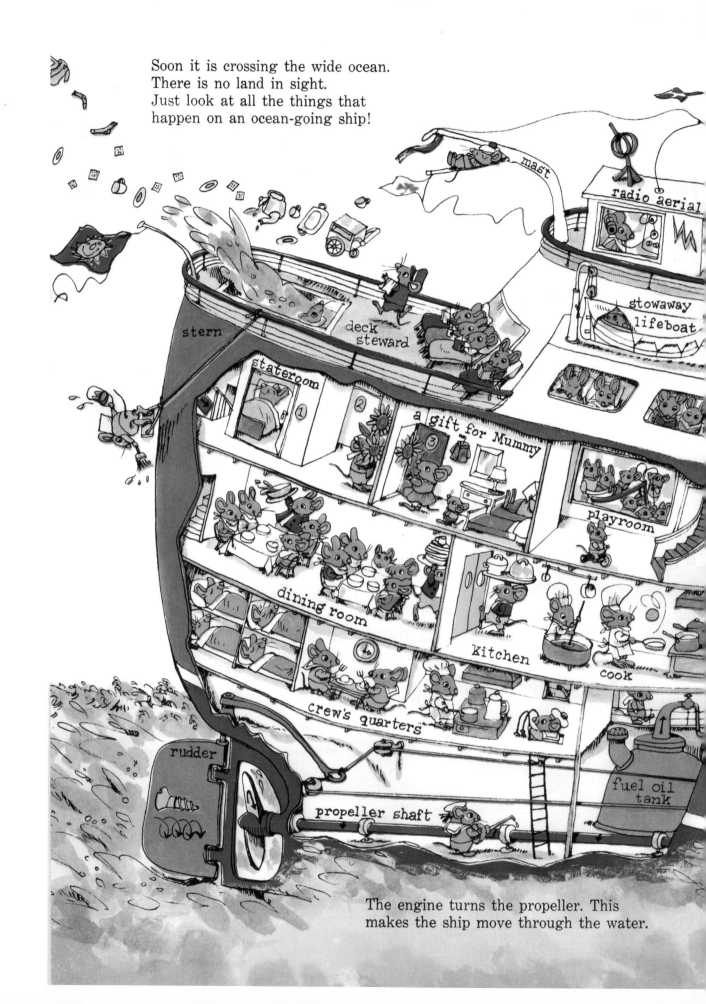

mast

radio aerial

stowaway

lifeboat

stern

deck
steward

stateroom

a gift for Mummy

playroom

dining room

kitchen

cook

crew's quarters

fuel oil
tank

rudder

propeller shaft

The engine turns the propeller. This
makes the ship move through the water.

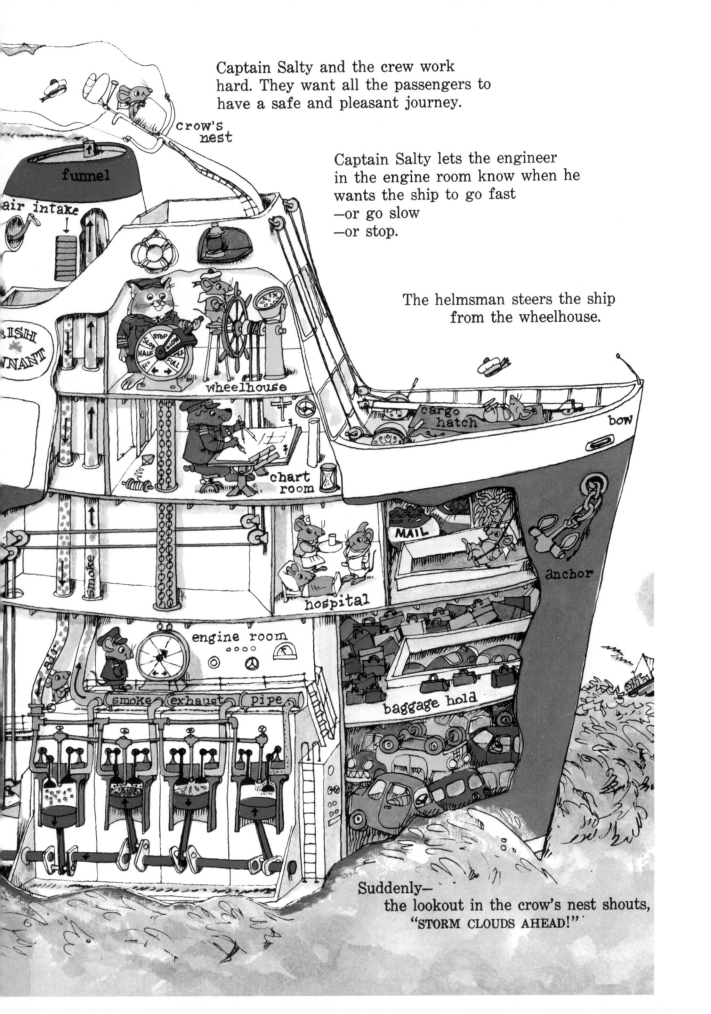

Captain Salty and the crew work
hard. They want all the passengers to
have a safe and pleasant journey.

Captain Salty lets the engineer
in the engine room know when he
wants the ship to go fast
—or go slow
—or stop.

The helmsman steers the ship
from the wheelhouse.

crow's
nest

funnel

air intake

wheelhouse

cargo
hatch

bow

chart
room

MAIL

anchor

smoke

hospital

engine room

smoke exhaust pipe

baggage hold

Suddenly—
    the lookout in the crow's nest shouts,
        "STORM CLOUDS AHEAD!"

Mixing Colours

Huckle will now show how to mix
two colours together to make a third colour!
Begin, Huckle!

Worm

Red → Orange ← Yellow

Red mixed with yellow makes orange.

Frog

Yellow → Green ← Blue

Yellow and blue make green.

Lizard

Red → Violet or Purple ← Blue

Red and blue make violet or purple.

Snail

Red → Pink ← White

Red and white make pink.

Fish

White → Grey ← Black

White and black make grey.

You are a fine colour mixer, Huckle.
Now, will YOU be able to remember how
to mix colours the next time you paint?
Of course, you will!

48

by Huck Scarry

"Where do you find the ideas for your books?" was no doubt the most frequent question my father heard. "Outside... in the street!" was his answer. Indeed, Richard was a funny man, and so he naturally saw all kinds of funny things going on around him. Little everyday mishaps were a source of ideas and amusing details to make his books the great fun that they are.

"Do you test your books on children?" was another frequent question. "Oh, never!" he would laugh. Richard simply put in his books the things that HE wanted to see there. When asked his age, he would put up one hand with spread fingers: "Five!" This wasn't all in jest, for my father, although a wise and intelligent man had the good sense never to lose the child within him. He always saw the world around him with exuberance and curiosity, as if for the very first time.

Of course, Richard was also an extremely gifted illustrator. I don't think there was ANYTHING he wasn't able to draw. And his earlier work, done in a more painterly fashion, shows an amazing capacity for handling watercolours, as well as a passion for treating his subjects with correctness and detail. Later, Richard abandoned treating his illustrations as paintings, and instead, did them as pen—and later as pencil drawings, which he subsequently coloured in. This was much more practical when his pages were packed with loads of characters and events. Once he had presented a new book to his editor, sketched out on sheets of tracing paper with bits of typed text taped to it, Richard would begin his pencil drawings. These were done on frosted acetate, similar in look to tracing paper, but less prone to tears, watermarks and creases.

When the book was completely drawn, all the illustrations would go to the photoengraver, who would make black-line films of them, for printing. These films were ALSO used to make a printing in very pale blue ink on illustration paper or board, on which my father could paint-in the colours, using the pale blue lines as guidelines. These printed blue lines are what this technique—"Blueboards" derives its name from.

Colouring-in a large book was always a long affair. I remember giving my father a hand with this sometimes. We would work together for a couple of weeks colouring a book, first starting with everything that ought to be red, then yellow, then orange, then blue, and so on, until each spread was absolutely complete. Or so we thought... browsing through his books today, I sometimes catch an unpainted bunny's paw that we missed!

Richard always used Winsor & Newton designer's colours, which he handled with great freedom depending on the effects he wanted—be it rich and opaque, say for clothes and cars, watery and splashy for lively skies or water, or bold 'dry' strokes for shadow or "speeding" effects. This variety in treatment makes his illustrations so much fun for the eye, and gives a lighthearted, spontaneous feeling to them.

And yet each was very cleverly and skillfully designed. Anyone who has ever tried to make a cutaway drawing of an airliner, a steamship, or a windmill can only marvel at how brilliantly my father could do this sort of thing!

His pages, bubbling with so many things to look at, are designed with a simple trick he learned from his very favourite painter, Peter Breughel: in many of Breughel's paintings, the viewer sits slightly aloft, as if atop a huge horse. This "cavaliere" viewpoint, looking downwards, reduces the perspective and allows each character on the painting, or page, be he or she way up at the more distant top, or down at the closer bottom, to catch your attention with equal strength. Our eyes, and imagination, are kept very, very BUSY!

Clang! Clang! Clang!
The firemen rushed to the fire.
They raised the ladder on the ladder truck.
A fireman ran up the ladder to rescue Mummy.
"SAVE MY HUCKLE!" she screamed.

water hydrant

Water is used to put fires out.
The water runs through pipes under the street.
The firemen attached a hose between the
water hydrant and the pumper engine.
The pumper engine got water from the hydrant
and squirted it out through the hose nozzle.

But the ladder wasn't
long enough to reach Huckle
up in the playroom!
How will they ever save him?

Brian Wildsmith

Brian Wildsmith is part of a group of illustrators who, in the revolution of the early 1960s, changed how picture-books were produced, enjoyed and absorbed.

Growing up in a small mining village in Yorkshire, Wildsmith turned to art and illustration to inject some colour into his grey surroundings. A scholarship allowed him to study at the Slade School of Art, but he was disillusioned with the teaching methods, which he felt inhibited individual creativity. Wildsmith has always believed in the importance of artistic expression, and his work reflects this. His first job as an illustrator were covers for Oxford University Press, and his first colour assignment was work for an edition of *Tales from the Arabian Nights*. Wildsmith's bold style was met with harsh criticism; one paper described his drawings as "pointless scribbles". Wildsmith was crushed, and thought his career as an illustrator was over. However, a friend from Oxford University Press told Wildsmith to pick himself up, and suggested he produce an alphabet book; the result was *Brian Wildsmith's ABC*.

Brian Wildsmith's ABC was groundbreaking, and Wildsmith himself has said of its impact "The *ABC* was the beginning of the picture-book revolution", and the book won the 1962 Kate Greenaway Medal.

Artwork from *Professor Noah's Spaceship* by Brian Wildsmith, illustration © Brian Wildsmith 1980, used by permission of Oxford University Press.

'Oh dear,'
said Professor Noah.
'One of our time guidance
fins has been damaged
on take-off. Soon we must
travel through a time-zone
which will take us
hundreds of years into
the future and help us
reach our new planet.
Our time-zone guidance
fin must be in the
correct position.
I need a strong volunteer
to go into space and twist
the fin back into shape.'
'I'll go,' said Elephant.
He put on a special
space-suit, went out
through the air-lock,
and pulled the fin into shape.
'Hurray!' they all shouted.
Professor Noah gave him
ten oranges and called
him a hero.

The way in which picture-books could be presented changed forever, as did the creative scope with which illustrators could produce their work. Illustration was opened up to include painting, collage and abstract art. Whilst making the book Wildsmith drew straight onto the page and painted the image in gouache.

Wildsmith's books often attempt to inspire in children a desire to help others and to reconnect children with nature, making them aware of our responsibility for the world around us. *Professor Noah's Spaceship*, 1980, was an early pioneer of environmentalism, where Noah herds the animals into a spaceship as Earth becomes victim to changing climatic conditions. Their journey through space takes them back in time, and they land on an Earth that is as yet unspoilt by man; the animals pledge to keep it that way. Wildsmith's championing of the environment as well as the use of Biblical influences was continued with other titles such as his pop-up book *The Creation*.

Through his work, Wildsmith hopes to inspire children to take an interest in art themselves, and use it to express their own individuality and feelings. He believes that great picture-books can shape a child's ability to see and think visually, and that this skill will manifest itself in later life. His influence on modern illustration has earned him a reputation as one of the greatest living illustrators.

Above Artwork from *Professor Noah's Spaceship* by Brian Wildsmith, illustration © Brian Wildsmith 1980.
Opposite top Artwork from *The Creation* by Brian Wildsmith, illustration © Brian Wildsmith 1995.
Opposite bottom Artwork from *Brian Wildsmith's ABC* by Brian Wildsmith, illustration © Brian Wildsmith 1962.
All images used by permission of Oxford University Press.

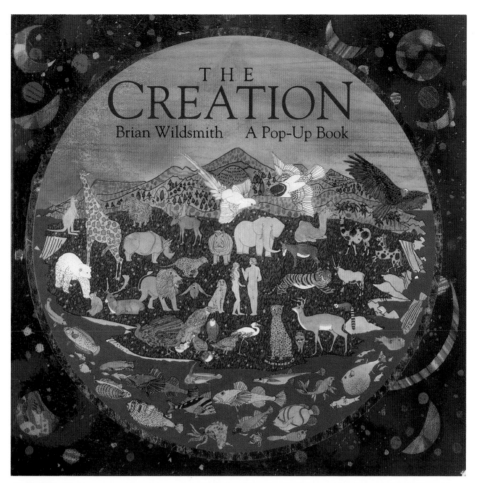

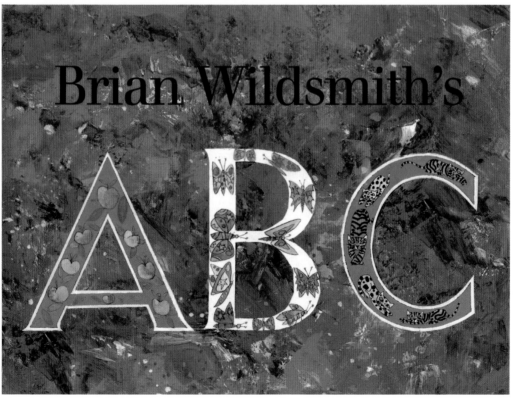

Afterwords

Contemporary Children's Books

Essay Notes

1 Glover, M, "Capturing the Bear Essentials of Paddington", Times Online, May 7 2008, accessed 26/06/09.

2 Lewis, D, *Reading Contemporary Picture Books: Picturing Text*, London and New York: Routledge/Falmer, 2001, p. xiii.

3 Travis, M, "Bursting with Joy: Interview with Brian Wildsmith", Booktrust Children's Books Website, 2008, accessed 27/06/09.

4 Martin, D, *The Telling Line*, London: Julia MacRae Books, 1989.

5 Sendak, M, *Caldecott & Co.: Notes on Books & Pictures*, London: Reinhardt Books, 1989, p. 209.

6 Sendak, *Caldecott & Co.*, p. 171

7 Sendak, *Caldecott & Co.*, p. 21

8 Higonnet, MR, "The Playground of the Peritext", Children's Literature in Education, Vol. 15, No. 2, Summer 1990, pp. 47–49.

9 Sendak, *Caldecott & Co.*, p8.

10 Ormerod, J, "The Inevitability of Transformation: Designing Picture Books for Children and Adults", Morag Styles, *After Alice*, London: Cassell, 1992, pp. 42–55.

11 Sendak, *Caldecott & Co.*, p. 52.

12 Pullman, P, "Picture Stories and Graphic Novels", K Reynolds and N Tucker, *Children's Book Publishing in Britain Since 1945*, Aldershot: Ashgate Publishing, 1998, pp. 110–132.

13 Moss, E, "Raymond Briggs: On British attitudes to the strip cartoon and children's-book illustration", *Signal 28*, January 1979, pp. 26–33.

14 Gallaz, Christophe: 1985; translation Ian McEwan, 1985.

15 Salisbury, M, *Illustrating Children's Books: Creating Pictures for Publication*, London: A&C Black, 2004, p. 95.

References

Booktrust

Booktrust is an independent charity dedicated to encouraging people of all ages and cultures to engage with books. The written word underpins the charity's activity and enables them to fulfil its vision of inspiring a lifelong love of books for all. Booktrust is responsible for a number of successful national reading promotions, sponsored book prizes and creative reading projects aimed at encouraging readers to discover and enjoy books. These include the Orange Prize for Fiction, the Children's Laureate, the Get London Reading campaign, the Booktrust Teenage Prize and Bookstart, the national programme that works through locally-based organisations to give a free pack of books to young children, with guidance materials for parents and carers.

As a non-profit making organisation, with strong links to the publishing industry, Booktrust was in a key position to champion the cause of the picture-book and the talented illustrators who historically have found it difficult to secure the celebrated reputation their work undoubtedly deserves.

The Big Picture campaign was created by Booktrust in 2007 to introduce picture-books to new audiences, elevate their reputation and generate interest in illustration as an art form in its own right.

The Big Picture's quest to find an exciting, new generation of illustrators was launched by Michael Rosen in September 2007; the response from publishers was overwhelming with over 200 picture books arriving at the Booktrust offices. Entrants had to have been first published in the UK in or since 2000, but all illustrative styles and techniques were welcomed. A longlist of 27 names, all thought to reflect a fresh approach to the picture-book tradition, was put together by members of Booktrust's children's books team and representative books from each illustrator were duly sent out to the judging panel.

As the campaign progresses, Booktrust is hopeful that the audience and appreciation for picture-books will continue to flourish, and build on the buzz and unprecedented media coverage that has already been established in the initial stages of the campaign. Specifically, the need to celebrate the established figures in illustration and continue to celebrate and highlight the tremendous artistic works of the ten best new illustrators, to encourage audiences to take risks with their book buying and become more familiar with the names of writers and illustrators who deserve to have widespread recognition of their talents, not only by children, but by adults too.

The search for the next generation of illustrators will launch in 2010.

www.booktrust.org.uk

The Ezra Jack Keats Foundation

The Ezra Jack Keats Foundation was established in 1964 with Keats as its President and Keats' great friend Martin Pope as its secretary. When Keats died in 1983, Pope became President and developed a number of programmes through which the royalties from Keats' works could be used to encourage children's involvement with books, and to nurture new talent.

The Ezra Jack Keats 'New Writer' and 'New Illustrator' awards are given annually to new talents that are recognised by the Foundation as showing outstanding skills in writing and illustrating, and to honour the authors and illustrators who continue to create children's books in the spirit of Keats. The award is presented jointly by the Foundation and the New York Public Library.

The Ezra Jack Keats Foundation also encourages the study of Keats' work through their Keats Fellowship, a scholarly award that supports the study of the de Grummond collection which is held at the McCain Library in the University of Southern Mississippi and is an archive including many of Keats' original illustrations as well as work from over 1,200 other authors and illustrators. The Keats Fellowship gives scholars grants of up to $1,200.

More information on the Ezra Jack Keats Foundation is available on their website, which includes examples of Keats' artwork, animated read aloud versions of a number of his books, as well as further information on the various programmes supported.

www.ezra-jack-keats.org

Seven Stories

Seven Stories, the Centre for Children's Books, is located in Newcastle upon Tyne and is the first museum in the UK wholly dedicated to the art of British children's books and takes its name from the idea that there are only seven stories in the world being told over and over again. Supported by patrons including Quentin Blake, Philip Pullman and Jacqueline Wilson, Seven Stories is building up an archive of artwork and manuscripts showcasing the processes behind beloved children's books. One of the earliest acquisitions was the archive and book collection of Kaye Webb, Puffin editor and founder of the Puffin Club; researchers pore over diaries, scrapbooks and correspondence, including letters to authors such as Joan Aiken, creator of *Arabel and Mortimer*. Treasures of the collection include Ruth Gervis' original drawings for her sister Noel Streatfield's novel *Ballet Shoes* in 1936, Nick Sharratt's rough sketches and artwork for *Starring Tracy Beaker*, and manuscripts from the *His Dark Materials* trilogy donated by Philip Pullman. The Collection currently includes original work by over 70 children's authors and illustrators, from the 1930s to the present day and hosts an exciting programme of exhibitions, arts and education events and activities.

Seven Stories is a registered charity and relies on grants and voluntary donations. Registered charity number 1056812, supported by Arts Council England and Newcastle City Council.

www.sevenstories.org.uk

The Osborne Collection of Early Children's Books

Now containing over 80,000 titles, the Osborne Collection, held at Toronto Public Library, began in 1949 with a donation of 2,000 books from British Librarian Edgar Osborne, intended as a research collection in children's literature. The donation was prompted by Osborne's visit to Toronto's public libraries 15 years earlier, when he was deeply impressed by the range and calibre of services for children. The collection now includes book related art, literary archives, games and ephemera, ranging from cuneiform tablets from 2000 BC to contemporary books selected to be part of the collection. The archive boasts a fourteenth century manuscript of Aesop's Fables, as well as both Florence Nightingale and Queen Mary's childhood libraries.

www.torontopubliclibrary.ca

Wandsworth Collection of Early Children's Books

In 1959 Wandsworth acquired a small private collection of early children's books. This was of some importance since the Osborne Collection (one of the largest and most important British collections) had gone to Toronto and there were few other collections available to the public in this country. The then Senior Children's Librarian, Mrs Doris Aubrey, was instrumental in its purchase and under her guidance Wandsworth was able to add to this nucleus. From the beginning the collection was developed to represent the growth of children's literature and of publishing for children through the eighteenth, nineteenth and early twentieth centuries. This has resulted in a collection that ranges from novels to annuals, picture-books to educative texts and novelty books to tracts. While the earliest items date from 1673 and there is a small but interesting selection of books pre-1850, the bulk of the books—as might be expected—cover the period 1850–1959.

At the beginning the records were kept on cards. However, in 1972 a published catalogue was produced. This was soon felt to be inadequate and a complete revision was undertaken and the new edition appeared in 1997. Since then acquisitions have been added to the Wandsworth online catalogue. The collection, itself, has had to move several times. Originally housed at Battersea District Library, it was transferred to West Hill before finding a permanent home in Putney Library where it is housed in its own purpose built room. It is now looked after by Ferelith Hordon and though not open to the general public, it is available for study by appointment.

www.wandsworth.gov.uk

A Big Thank You

In *Illustrated Children's Books* a debt of gratitude must be made to the following people who put in their time, advice and contributed their artwork to this book, celebrating the literary and artistic form of this fascinating and complex medium. First and foremost, thank you to Ferelith Hordon at the Wandsworth Collection of Early Children's books, whose patience and enthusiasm contributed to our first excitement in exploring the world of children's illustrated literature —we hope that the snakes come in handy. A big thank you to Philip Pullman whose advice at the beginning led us to the two fantastic contributors to the book; Peter Hunt and Lisa Sainsbury, whose expertise in their essays lead us through the cornucopia of illustrated children's books from Comenius to the present day. Their efforts are much appreciated. Thank you to Leslie McGrath at the Osborne Collection of Early Children's Books in Toronto Public Library for giving her time and to Hannah Green at the Seven Stories Collection, the Centre for Children's Books in Newcastle, for sharing the original artwork of the celebrated illustrators featured here, of whom Shirley Hughes, John Lawrence, Pat Hutchins, Robert Crowther, Judith Kerr, and the estate of Edward Ardizzone, kindly allowed us to reproduce their work. We would not without the collaboration of artists, publishers and agents have been able to show the wealth of work displayed here, thank you to John Williamson at Walker Books, Dominic Kingston at Macmillan, Jessica Halliwell at Frances Lincoln, Gabrielle White at Random House, Mathilde Coffy at Anderson Press, Deborah Pope at the Ezra Jack Keats Foundation, Alison Vellacott at Highlight PR, Kate Johnson at Georges Borchardt, June Holmes at the Natural History Society of Northumbria, Bill McLoughlin and Audrey Mooney at DC Thomson, Heather Birchall at the Whitworth Art Gallery, Moira Allen editor of Mostly-Victorian.com, Henry Brooke, Gordon Dickerson, Angela Dixon, Paddy Bannerman, Huck Scarry, the family of John Ryan and finally to those artists who contributed freely to the book; Michael Foreman, Dick Bruna, Robert Sabuda, Val Biro, Posy Simmonds, Helen Craig, Jan Ormerod, Jan Pieńkowski, Mini Grey, Graham Rawle, Christian Birmingham, Marcia Williams, Polly Dunbar, Sara Fanelli, Emily Gravett, Eric Carle, Dave McKean, Chris Riddell, Helen Oxenbury, Lucy Cousins, Shirley Hughes, Alexis Deacon, John Burningham, Anthony Browne, Jessica Ahlberg, Axel Scheffler and Julia Donaldson.

Thank you to Anthony Browne for contributing his work and writing the Foreword and to Katherine Solomon at Booktrust. A special thanks to Libby Waite, Kate Trant, Huck Scarry, Deborah Pope, Brooke Sperry, Marie Le Clerc, Maria Sell, Esther Croom, Becky Hallam, Ben Jeffery, Matt Bucknall, Matt Pull, Johanna Bonnevier, Emily Chicken, Live Bergitte Molvær, Alex Wright and Rachel Pfleger, without whom this book would not have been possible.

Sophie Hallam

Front Cover Illustrations (clockwise from top)

•From *Miffy's Dream* by Dick Bruna Illustrations © Mercis bv 1953–2009.
•From *A Book of Nonsense* by Edward Lear. Courtesy of The Wandsworth Collection.
•From *The Golliwogg's Circus* written by Bertha Upton and illustrated by Florence K Upton. Courtesy of The Wandsworth Collection.
•From *Pugwash Aloft* by John Ryan, text and illustrations copyright © John Ryan 1958. First published by Frances Lincoln 2008.
•From *Alice's Adventures in Wonderland* written by Lewis Carroll and illustrated by John Tenniel. First published 1865.
•From *The Story of Babar* by Jean de Brunhoff. First published 1931.
•From *Tim in Danger*, text and illustrations © Edward Ardizzone 1953. First published Francis Lincoln 2006.
•From *Alice's Adventures in Wonderland* written by Lewis Carroll and illustrated by John Tenniel. First published 1865.
•From *Johnny Crow's Gardens* by LL Brooke. Courtesy of The Wandsworth Collection, reproduced by permission of Henry Brooke.
•From *Pugwash Aloft* by John Ryan, text and illustrations copyright © John Ryan 1958. First published by Frances Lincoln 2008.

Back Cover Illustration (clockwise from top)

•From *The Golliwogg's Circus* written by Bertha Upton and illustrated by Florence K Upton. Courtesy of The Wandsworth Collection.
•From *Alice's Adventures in Wonderland* written by Lewis Carroll and illustrated by John Tenniel. First published 1865. Courtesy of The Wandsworth Collection
•From *Oranges and Lemons* by LL Brooke. Courtesy of The Wandsworth Collection of The Wandsworth Collection.
•From *Mog the Forgetful Cat* by Judith Kerr. Illustrations © Kerr-Kneale Productions 1970.
•From *The Golliwogg's Circus* written by Bertha Upton and illustrated by Florence K Upton. Courtesy of The Wandsworth Collection of The Wandsworth Collection.
•From *The Bluebeard Picture Book* by Walter Crane, printed in colour by Edmund Evans. Reproduced courtesy of The Wandsworth Collection.

Title Page Illustration

From Richard Scarry's *What Do People Do All Day?* by Richard Scarry, © 1968 Richard Scarry, © renewed 1996 by Richard Scarry II. Used by permission of Random House Children's Books, a division of Random House, Inc. Reprinted by permission of HarperCollins Publishers Ltd.

Break Page Illustrations (in order of apperance)

•*The English Struwwelpeter or Pretty Stories and Funny Pictures* by Heinrich Hoffmann. All images courtesy of The Wandsworth Collection.
•Original illustration © 1986 Pat Hutchins from *1 Hunter*, courtesy of the Seven Stories Collection.
•Illustration © Mercis bv 1953–2009 from *Miffy is Crying* by Dick Bruna.

The End

Illustration from *The Story of Babar* by Jean de Brunhoff. First published 1931.

Edited by Duncan McCorquodale, Sophie Hallam and Libby Waite at Black Dog Publishing.
Designed by Matt Bucknall and Johanna Bonnevier at Black Dog Publishing.
Cover design by Live Bergitte Molvær at Black Dog Publishing.

Black Dog Publishing Limited
10a Acton Street
London WC1X 9NG
United Kingdom

Tel: +44 (0)20 7713 5097
Fax: +44 (0)20 7713 8682
info@blackdogonline.com
www.blackdogonline.com

ISBN 978 1 906155 81 0

British Library Cataloguing-in-Publication Data.
A CIP record for this book is available from the British Library.

Black Dog Publishing Limited, London, UK, is an environmentally responsible company. *Illustrated Children's Books* is printed on an FSC certified paper.

architecture art design
fashion history photography
theory and things

black dog publishing
london uk

www.blackdogonline.com